500 THINGS TO DO IN HOUSTON FOR FREE

including Galveston

by JOEL & PEGGY BLOOM

FOLLETT PUBLISHING COMPANY
CHICAGO

Cover design: **Joe Mistak**
Interior design: **MacDonald Graphics**
Typesetting: **Hagle**

Jim Hargrove Book Productions, Ltd.

Copyright © 1981 Jim Hargrove Book Productions, Ltd. All rights reserved. No portion of this book may be used or reproduced in any manner whatsoever without written permission from the publisher except in the case of brief quotations embodied in critical reviews and articles. Manufactured in the United States of America.

Library of Congress Cataloging in Publication Data

Bloom, Joel A.
  500 things to do in Houston for free.

    Includes index.
    1. Houston, Tex.—Description—Guide-books.
2. Galveston—Description—Guide-books. I. Bloom, Peggy, joint author. II. Title.
F394.H83B56 917.64'139 80-28267
ISBN 0-695-81563-6

First Printing

contents

Acknowledgments	9
1. Mud, Mosquitoes, and the Moon	11
2. Nature's Bounty	16
Armand Bayou Wilderness Preserve	17
Bay Area Park Boat Ride	18
Bear Creek Park	18
Big Creek Scenic Area	19
Big Thicket National Preserve	19
Edith Moore Sanctuary	20
Houston Arboretum and Botanical Gardens	21
Houston Garden Center and Rose Gardens	22
Houston Zoological Gardens	22
Lake Houston and Trinity River Dam	24
Mercer Arboretum	25
R. A. Vines Environmental Science Center	25
U.S. NATIONAL FOREST AND RECREATION AREAS	

Angelina National Forest	25
Davy Crockett National Forest	26
Sam Houston National Forest	28
TEXAS STATE PARKS	
Varner-Hogg Plantation State Park	29
Washington-on-the-Brazos State Park	29

3. Museums and Collections   30

Bayou Bend Collection of the Museum of Fine Arts	30
Blaffer Gallery	31
Brazosport Museum of Natural History	32
Burke Baker Planetarium	32
Contemporary Arts Museum	33
Fort Bend County Museum	34
Geophysical Society of Houston Museum	34
Gulf Coast Railroad Museum	34
The Houston Baseball Museum	34
Houston Heritage Society	35
Houston Public Library	38
Museum of American Architecture and Decorative Arts	38
Museum of Fine Arts	38
Museum of Medical Science	39
Museum of Natural Science	40
O'Kane Gallery	41
Pasadena Historical Museum	41
Rice University Museum	42
Rothko Chapel	42
Sam Houston Memorial Museum	43
San Jacinto Battleground	43
San Jacinto Monument and Museum of Texas History	43
U.S.S. Texas Battleship	45

4. Houston Parks and Recreation 46

Highlights of the biggest, newest, and best city parks are followed by exertrails, bikeways, gymnasiums, recreation centers, classes, swimming pools, and tennis courts.

5. Special Places 65

American Red Cross—Harris County Chapter	66
Anheuser-Busch	66
Annunciation Church	66
Antioch Baptist Church	66
Barker's Dam Telescope Tour	67
Cemeteries	67
Christ Church Cathedral	68
Coca-Cola Bottling Plant	69
Crispin Building	69
Farmer's Market Cooperative	69
The Galleria	69
Goodwill Industries	70
The Hanging Tree	71
Hilltop Herb Farm	71
Houston Fire Department	71
Imperial Sugar	72
Kennedy Trading Post	72
Houston Underground Tunnel System	72
Historic Downtown Buildings	74
Intercontinental Airport	77
Lyndon B. Johnson Space Center	77
The Medical Center	81
Newspaper Tours	82
Old Market Square	82
Old Sixth Ward—Sabine Historic District	82
Pennzoil Place	82

Pioneer Memorial Log House 83
Port of Houston 83
Post Oak Central, I, II 84
Sauer's Sausage Company 84
Shopping Centers 84
Society for the Prevention of Cruelty to Animals 87
Voluntary Action Center of Houston and Harris County 88
William F. Hobby Airport 89

6. The Libraries: City and County 90

The Central Library 90
Branch Libraries 92
Harris County Libraries 93
Clayton Library 94

7. Universities, Galleries, and Outdoor Art 96

A cultural crazy quilt of campus walking tours, art exhibits, outdoor sculptures, monuments, and fountains

8. Music, Films, and Plays 112

A short but sweet look at Houston's impressive free musical and screen offerings, with a coda for the immortal Bard

9. Annual Dos 116

A month-by-month summary of yearly free events

10. Historic Galveston — 126

PLACES TO VISIT IN GALVESTON
American National Insurance Company Tower — 128
Bolivar Ferry — 129
East End Historic District — 129
Galveston Beaches — 130
Galveston County Historical Museum — 132
Mosquito Fleet — 132
Rosenburg Library — 133
The Seawall — 133
The Strand — 133
Texas Heroes Monument — 135

OUTDOOR ACTIVITIES IN GALVESTON
Shelling and Beachcombing — 136
Saltwater Fishing — 138
Bird-watching — 138

Photo Credits — 139

Index — 141

To our family

acknowledgments

In researching a book like *500 Things to Do in Houston for Free*, it is impossible to dig out the necessary facts for all the places found without the assistance of knowledgeable people. We would like to acknowledge the helpfulness and expertise of those individuals. Special thanks to Joe Howard, Houston Parks and Recreation, and their photographer Scott Stone; Dale Bounds, National Forest Service; Mary Anita Paddock, Houston Convention and Visitors Council; Susan Ray Permenter, Galveston Visitors Center; Mrs. Glasser, Houston Public Library; and Barry Klein, Greater Houston Preservation Alliance.

In addition, we would like to thank the public relations people at the following institutions for their greatly appreciated efforts: The Museum of Natural History, The Museum of Medical Science, The Houston Museum of Fine Arts, The Contemporary Arts Museum, The Heritage Society, The Houston Baseball Museum, The University of Houston, Rice University, Houston Baptist University, St. Thomas University, and Texas Southern University. Without the combined efforts of these people, this venture would have been impossible.

CHAPTER 1

mud, mosquitoes, and the moon

In 1836 the land situated at the headland of navigation on the western portion of Buffalo Bayou was infested with mosquitoes, mudflats, and tangled undergrowth. Hardly the setting for what was to become a futuristic city of gleaming towers, industry, and economic prosperity and an integral part of the United States' exploration of the moon.

The "energy capital of the world" began as the concept of two brothers, J. K. and A. C. Allen, real estate promoters from New York. They paid $9,428 for 6,642 acres of land and Houston was on its way. The town was named to honor their hero and good friend, General Sam Houston, whose undermanned band of Texans had recently defeated General Santa Anna's Mexican army at San Jacinto, just a few miles away. The Allen brothers were certain that their personal friend would become the first President of the Texas Republic and that he would select Allen's Landing, now named Houston, as their capital. This became a reality and Houston remained the capital until 1839, when President Mirabeau B. Lamar moved the government to Waterloo, Texas, which was to become Austin, named for Stephen F. Austin, the "father of Texas." This move temporarily stunted Houston's

growth, but the city's adolescence was just around the corner.

As the turn of the century approached, Houston began to take shape as a port for Stephen F. Austin's colony. In 1837, the *Laura* became the first steamship to visit Houston, traveling 15 miles from Harrisburg in three days. This navigational feat—cruising through winding Buffalo Bayou—designated the town as the Port of Houston. In 1844, the large steamboat *Constitution* anchored at the port. Even though the ship had to be backed down the bayou to a wider point to turn around for its return trip, its arrival gave a great boost to Houston's fledgling commerce.

In 1846 Texas became the 28th star in the U.S. flag, and in 1853 the railroad came to Houston. With rail service and the Port of Houston increasing in importance, industry came to the young city, bringing an iron foundry and a large warehouse system for cotton, hides, and various other commodities. By 1856 Main Street had been surfaced with shell, rail service was rolling between Houston and Galveston on the Galveston-Houston and Red River Railroad, the city had dredged and deepened Buffalo Bayou, and prosperity was evident and seemed permanent.

The discovery of oil at Spindletop in 1901 began a new era in Houston's growth. World War I and the rising momentum of the auto industry saw Texas and Houston at the center of this new industrial effort. The city became known as the point "where seventeen railways meet the sea." Its economic importance continued to blossom. The railroads transported the black gold and refineries and other petroleum-related plants clustered the area. Strongly identified with the oil industry, Houston increased in population as the major oil companies established their headquarters in the city and became involved in offshore drilling and worldwide production.

In the 1950s and 1960s the economy of the area began to change again as industry and business diversified. Air conditioning made the hot, humid summer livable, and the location of NASA's Lyndon B. Johnson Space Center put Houston on the map of the world.

"Houston—the Eagle has landed." The world now knew where Houston was and the city rapidly became the center of space technology, science, and knowledge. Paralleling this effort was the development of the famed Texas Medical Center and the area's other major medical and health care facilities. Brilliant minds, skilled physicians, and creative researchers moved to Houston, drawing patients from all over the world as the renown of the center spread.

Houston is not only an industrial giant and health leader, but also a recognized mecca of culture. Today it boasts the nationally known Alley Theater, the Houston Symphony Orchestra, Houston Grand Opera, Houston

Ballet, and the Music Hall. Fine museums, galleries, art collections, and hundreds of other centers of the fine and performing arts enhance Houston's charm.

Houston is the city in the news; it's where the action is; it's a town where you might see people on horseback ride into a shopping center as well as in automobiles. It's a town of business clothes and western wear, of Tony Lama boots and Aigner shoes, of rodeos and tennis tournaments, horse shows and cultural parades. It has the lowest median age (27) of any major American city. It is vibrant, alive, and still growing. We have described Houston as the diamond in the buckle of the sunbelt.

With *500 Things to Do in Houston for Free* you can share in Houston's personality. You will find the information you need, including addresses (and general directions for a few sites that are outside of Greater Houston), to enjoy at least 500 significant and often educational experiences, all without charge. Many are bound to be just right for you and your interests. Where possible, you should call ahead to confirm the details presented here.

GETTING AROUND IN HOUSTON

Houston is designed mainly for automobile travel. To the uninitiated, traveling by car can take some practice. Since the city is not bounded by any natural barriers, such as mountains or bodies of water, Houston has, during its short history, managed to attain a considerable degree of urban sprawl in almost every direction. With a great many exceptions, roads generally run north and south and east and west, but because of an attempt by city planners to create a thoroughfare parallel to the Buffalo Bayou, most downtown streets are laid out in oblique directions.

A good city street map is indispensable. A high-quality road map offered exclusively to members of the American Automobile Association is virtually identical to Rand McNally's over-the-counter version. For the perfectionist, the *Key Map Book of Houston* offers the most detailed breakdown of city streets available anywhere, but the price is several times that of this volume.

The Metropolitan Transit Authority (Metro) operates dozens of bus routes that generally extend from the downtown districts into outlying areas. Detailed route maps, which also contain specific schedules for key stops along the route on weekdays and weekends, are available free of charge for each individual route. Copies can be found at major banks, museums, universities, and many other locations throughout the city. If all else fails and you are left with 500 places to see but not the slightest idea of how to get to them, try calling the Metro information hotline at 651-1212. Whoever answers the phone will make a gallant effort to answer your questions.

CHAPTER 2

nature's bounty

The sprawling asphalt and concrete thoroughfares of Houston are virtually surrounded by areas of natural beauty. Nearly a million acres of National Forests and other scenic areas are within a two-hour drive of the metropolitan area, generally to the north. To the south, miles and miles of open beaches along the Gulf of Mexico beckon to sunworshipers and fans of the sand and surf. (For a description of these areas around Galveston, see chapter 10.) Scattered throughout greater Houston are more than half a dozen lovely preserves dedicated to the flora and fauna of the Southwest.

If your time is limited, it may be difficult to choose from all the exciting possibilities. They include a free boat ride (two more are discussed in later chapters), a major zoological garden, more than 200 miles of wilderness hiking trails, free lectures and nature walks, botanic gardens, environmental centers, free state parks, canoe trails, picnic spots, great places to fish, and so much more.

If this embarrassment of riches doesn't make the decision-making process difficult enough, here is a way to add significantly to your list of things to do and places to visit. A large, 160-page, full-color book, entitled

Texas—Land of Contrast, describes many tourist attractions throughout the state, including some of the nature preserves and parks in the Houston area. The book can be obtained free of charge by writing to: State Department of Highways and Public Transportation, Travel and Information Division, P.O. Box 5064, Austin, TX 78763. In addition to listings of specific sites organized by region (in Texas, after all, there can be more than 800 miles between here and there), the book provides information on hunting and fishing regulations, rocks and minerals, flowers, and birds.

Armand Bayou Wilderness Preserve
8600 Bay Area Boulevard (off I-45 South)
Clear Lake City
474-2551
Only 20 miles south of downtown Houston, this preserve encompasses more than 2,000 acres of estuarine floodplain. The quiet, secluded hiking trails are kept that way by a dedicated staff that limits the number of walkers who may tour at any one time. The bayou itself offers a 12-mile stretch of water that can be explored in canoes. Self-guided tours may be taken between Tuesday and Sunday from 9 to 5. Free guided tours are conducted on Saturdays and Sundays at 10 and 2. The preserve is closed on Mondays and major holidays.

Owl Prowls—nighttime walks through the woods—begin at 7 P.M. (7:30 P.M. during June, July, and August) on the first and third Wednesdays of each month, except during December, January, and February. Lectures on special topics are held at various times throughout the year, but you can count on attending the Early Birding lectures at 7 A.M. on the first Saturday of each month. Schedules and topics for other lectures are published in local newspapers. The Armand Bayou Nature Center also conducts a number of classes for which there is a charge.

Nearly a million acres of preserves and forests are in or near Houston.

Bay Area Park Boat Ride
7500 Bay Area Boulevard
Clear Lake City
221-6126
A one-hour boat ride takes visitors down the Armand Bayou. Reservations must be made in advance through the county commissioner's office by calling the number above. (For information on other free boat rides in the Houston area, see Port of Houston in chapter 5 and Bolivar Ferry in chapter 10.)

Bear Creek Park
15115 Clay Road
More than 2,000 acres of recreational land include picnic and play areas, baseball and softball diamonds. (A fee is

charged to play on the golf course.) To reach the park, which is open daily, take I-10 West to the Addicks exit and proceed three miles north on State Highway 6.

Big Creek Scenic Area
9 miles southwest of Shepherd
A 3½-mile easy hiking trail winds through towering trees and along running streams. Much of the trail is on an old railroad tram (the tracks have been removed). No camping or picnicking is allowed at the 1,130-acre site, which has been preserved more or less in its natural state.

Located within the boundaries of the Sam Houston National Forest (described later in this chapter), the site is within easy hiking range of the Double Lake Recreation Area. Signs describing native flora and fauna are scattered throughout the preserve, which includes within its boundaries fragments of the famous Lone Star National Recreation Trail. For a free eight-page color brochure describing the area, write to: National Forests in Texas, Forest Supervisor, P.O. Box 969, Lufkin, TX 75901. Ask for the Big Creek Scenic Area brochure.

Big Thicket National Preserve
12 locations spread around southeast Texas
Kountze Visitor Information Center: 246-2337
During the latter half of 1980, the Big Thicket was a source of considerable controversy as environmentalists battled other interest groups to maintain the wilderness status of the widely scattered parcels of land now included in the National Preserve. Much of the land in the 12 separate units of Big Thicket, now operated by the National Park Service, is so densely packed with undergrowth that vast areas are virtually impenetrable. In some spots, flowing streams and marshes are almost hidden by the tangled woods.

The Big Thicket Visitor Information Station is located on FM 420 about five miles north of Kountze. Here, visitors

Rangers lead free guided canoe trips through Big Thicket National Preserve river bottoms.

can learn the details about various free monthly activities, such as guided canoe trips, beginners' bird walks, seasonal hikes, and photography and nature walks. Information on the preserve and a number of brochures describing self-guiding walks along widely scattered Big Thicket trails can be obtained at the same location. Fishing and walk-in camping are permitted, but a free camping permit should be obtained in person at the Kountze Visitor Information Center. Call ahead for hours.

Edith Moore Sanctuary—Houston Audubon Society
440 Wilchester
932-1392 (If no answer, call 228-0037.)
The 17-acre preserve includes several self-guiding nature trails and encompasses a small, unaltered portion of Rummel Creek. With 75 species of woody plants and 150 species of birds, this small island of ecological protection serves as a window onto Houston's forest community.

Trails are accessible from the parking lot of the Memorial Drive Methodist Church, 12955 Memorial Drive. The entrance sign to the sanctuary is at the north-

Visitors to Houston Arboretum and Botanical Gardens can enjoy miles of self-guiding trails.

west corner of the lot. The sanctuary cabin can be reached from the Wilchester entrance, just west of the church at 440 Wilchester. A must for anyone interested in ecology and conservation, the preserve is open daily until dusk.

Houston Arboretum and Botanical Gardens
4500 Woodway at I-610 (West Loop)
681-8433
Operated by the Houston Botanical Society, the Arboretum and Botanical Gardens serve as a sanctuary for trees and plants, a place where urbanites can recontact a natural environment. It is on a 256-acre site with five miles of trail systems for leisurely walking and viewing. May to October hours are 8:30 A.M. to 8 P.M. From November to April shortened hours are 8:30 to 6. Free guided tours are offered on Sundays at 1.

Houston Garden Center and Rose Gardens
1500 Hermann Drive (in Hermann Park)
529-5371

The highlight of these public gardens is a collection of more than 3,000 rose bushes, but there are a number of other impressive floral displays. The perennial garden is profuse with perennial flowers common to the Houston area. The fragrance garden features a special array of plants with distinct scents and textures. A number of weddings are held each year in the rose gardens. Best viewing is from April to November. Open daily from 8:30 A.M. to sunset.

Houston Zoological Gardens
Hermann Park at Fannin and Outer Belt Drive
522-0276

These 43 acres are home to nearly 2,000 animals. The collection includes amphibians, reptiles, birds, and mammals. Endangered species are of particular interest and are marked with signs. The brown pelican, Scimitar-horned oryx, and other endangered animals have been bred successfully by the Houston Zoo. Large protected areas for the animals' comfort simulate natural habitats. Admission and 1,200 parking spaces are free.

Summer Hours

Zoo Entrance: 9:30 A.M. to 8:00 P.M. daily.
Mammal House: 9:30 A.M. to 7:30 P.M. daily.
Reptile House: 9:30 A.M. to 7:30 P.M. Closed Wednesday afternoons.
Tropical Bird House: 10 A.M. to 4 P.M. Monday through Saturday; 10 A.M. to 5 P.M. Sunday.
Gorilla Habitat: 10 A.M. to 4 P.M. Monday through Saturday; 10 A.M. to 5 P.M. Sunday.
Children's Zoo: 10 A.M. to 4 P.M. Monday through Saturday; 10 A.M. to 5 P.M. Sunday.

Feeding Locations and Times

Vampire Bats: Small Mammal House Nocturnal Section, 2:30 P.M. daily.

Youngsters as well as the young at heart can pet and feed domestic and gentle wild animals in the 2-acre Children's Zoo. The New Houston Zoo facility is geographically oriented.

Sea Lions: Sea Lion Display at Zoo Entrance, 10 A.M. and 3 P.M. daily.
Alligators: Alligator Display behind the Reptile House, 2 P.M. Wednesdays and Sundays.

The Children's Zoo brings people and animals into close contact under supervised conditions. There are four contact areas and several low-fenced perimeter exhibits, a hatchery, an aquatunnel for observing aquatic life forms, and a facility for raising and displaying baby animals.

This cheetah is one of the thousands of animals living in a nearly natural environment at the Houston Zoological Gardens.

The zoo staff presents a number of free films and lectures for general audiences during midday periods. For specific information and times, call 522-7098. Stationed at major exhibits throughout the zoo, staff members are also available to provide additional information and answer questions about the animals and the zoo. The zoo office can be contacted by calling 523-0149 between 7:30 A.M. and 4:00 P.M.

Lake Houston and Trinity River Dam
Trinity River and Lake Livingston
Located about 50 miles north of downtown Houston on U.S. Highway 59, this very beautiful natural spot is the site of the Trinity River Dam on the San Jacinto River. Controlling the level of the two bodies of water and actually forming the lake, the Trinity Dam and Lake Livingston are instrumental in supplying Houston's water. Some areas are marked for boating and picnicking. Open daily.

Mercer Arboretum
22306 Aldine Westfield Road
Humble
443-8731
This small arboretum is about a 40-minute drive north of downtown Houston near the Intercontinental Airport. Here, three acres of landscaped gardens are nestled in a 12-acre tract of untouched woods. Self-guided tours can be taken Monday through Sunday from 8 to 5.

R. A. Vines Environmental Science Center
8856 Westview
465-9628
Home of more than 200 species of trees, shrubs, and vines native to Texas, the arboretum is on a five-acre site. All plants are labeled with their common and scientific names. Also on the grounds of the center are the Texas Hall of Zoology, Hall of Geology, Hall of Oceanography, and the Jack Roach Hall of Exotic Animals. Admission to all is, of course, free. Public hours are generally 8:30 to 4:30 on weekdays, but some exhibits are closed when classes are in session.

U.S. NATIONAL FOREST AND RECREATION AREAS

Angelina National Forest
Highway 63, about 20 miles east of Lufkin
Located approximately 100 miles northeast of Houston, this federally owned and protected area has more than 155,000 acres of rolling hills covered with pine and mixed hardwood trees. The principal recreation site is the Sam Rayburn Reservoir, where any type of boat, from a canoe to a cabin cruiser, is welcome to cruise the warm waters. Developed recreation areas are scattered along the seemingly endless shoreline. On the southwest bank are Sandy Creek, Caney Creek, and Letney. Townsend and Harvey Creek are on the northeast shore. Each of these areas has at least one free boat ramp, but as for all

National Forests in Texas, there is a small daily use fee for swimming at developed beaches and overnight camping at improved campsites. Visitors may swim at their own risk without charge anywhere outside of developed beaches.

The 5½-mile Saw Mill Hiking Trail connects the Bouton Lake Recreation Area (on Forest Service Road 303 about 15 miles southeast of Zavalla) with the Boykin Springs Recreation Area, passing by the ruins of the old Aldrich Sawmill. The designated trail is marked with triangular patches of white paint, and primitive camping is permitted free of charge along the entire route.

At the time of this writing, there are no public information brochures describing the Angelina National Forest, but a free eight-page directory of all the National Forest Recreational Areas in Texas, which includes color maps, can be obtained by writing to: National Forests in Texas, Forest Supervisor, P.O. Box 969, Lufkin, TX 75901. An extremely detailed Class A Map of the Angelina Forest is available for 50¢ by writing to the same address.

Davy Crockett National Forest
Due east of Crockett (about 110 miles north of Houston)
More than 160,000 acres of federal land affords plenty of elbow room to lovers of the great outdoors. The largest number of activity centers are located around Ratcliff on State Route 7 deep in the woods. Here you can have a picnic, ride in your motorless boat on Lake Ratcliff, hike along miles of heavily forested trails, and generally get away from it all. (As in all National Forests in Texas, some activities, including swimming at developed beaches and overnight camping in designated areas, have a small daily use fee.)

About ten miles east of Ratcliff, the Neches River, which marks the eastern boundary of the National Forest, meanders toward the Gulf of Mexico. Leading into the Neches River and continuing southward within its shores is the Big Slough Canoe Trail. It begins about six miles

The Big Slough Canoe Trail leads into the Neches River, which forms the eastern boundary of Davy Crockett National Forest.

north of Ratcliff on Forest Service Road 517A at Scurlock Camp, a primitive, free campground used for the canoe trail head. The slough portion of the trail is indicated by orange markers, but no markers are provided on the Neches River, which is easy enough to follow by flowing with the strong current. To take advantage of that current, travel the trail in a clockwise direction. The Big Slough Canoe Trail is best used during the winter and spring. During most of summer and fall the water level is too low for comfortable paddling.

The 4-C's National Recreational Trail is the longest in Crockett National Forest. The 19-mile trail begins at Ratcliff Lake Recreation Area (off State Highway 103) and terminates at Neches Bluff Overlook (south of State Highway 21). The only potable water along the entire trail is at Ratcliff, so fill your canteens and thermoses to the brim. Primitive year-round camping all along the trail is free. For a free map of the trail, write to: Davy Crockett National Forest, East Loop 304, Crockett, TX 75835. Ask for the 4-C's National Recreation Trail Map. By writing to the same address, you can also obtain free copies of brochures describing the recreational facilities at Ratcliff Lake as well as information on Big Slough Canoe Trail. Be sure to specify which publications you wish to receive. By enclosing 50¢, you can also get a detailed map of the entire forest. Ask for the Class A Map of Davy Crockett National Forest.

Sam Houston National Forest
Approximately 65 miles north of Houston off I-45
344-6205 or 344-6958
For work-weary Houstonians, the National Forest nearest the metropolitan area is a popular weekend getaway spot (if a 160,000-acre forest can be called a spot). The 140-mile Lone Star Hiking Trail is one of the area's premier attractions. Trails can be found near Double Lake (five miles south of Coldspring), Stubblefield Lake (on the west fork of the San Jacinto River about 12 miles north-

west of New Waverly), and in the Big Creek Scenic Area (approximately eight miles south of Coldspring).

Little Lake Creek on Route 149 in the southern portion of the forest (near Montgomery) is a proposed National Wilderness Area of about 2,300 acres. Several free motorcycle trails were opened to the public in late 1980. Hunting is permitted in season. For details, check with the Texas Parks and Wildlife Department in Houston (phone: 443-0946).

A free map and brochure, *Guide to Hiking the Lone Star Trail*, can be obtained by writing to: Sam Houston National Forest, P.O. Box 393, New Waverly, TX 77358. A detailed Class A map can also be ordered from the same address by enclosing 50¢. Ranger stations are located in the towns of Cleveland and New Waverly.

TEXAS STATE PARKS

Varner-Hogg Plantation State Park
West Columbia, State Highway 35
Located about a 45-minute drive south of Houston off State Highway 288, this plantation home was built in 1836 and was owned by Governor James S. Hogg between 1901 and 1906. The spacious grounds are ideal for relaxed strolling and gracious picnicking. Entry to the park grounds is free, but there is a charge to tour the interior of the mansion. Closed on Mondays and Tuesdays.

Washington-on-the Brazos State Park
East of Brenham on FM 1155 (From I-10 West)
Although there is an admission fee to enter the star shaped museum within the park, the grounds themselves are worth seeing. Extensive landscaping projects have re-created the flora common to the area in 1836. Large picnic groves are located along the Brazos, and a number of pioneer homes and shops have been restored. Closed Mondays and Tuesdays.

CHAPTER 3

museums and collections

Amid the bustle of Houston's life-style are more than 20 placid reminders of the city's colorful past and promising future. Ranging in size from small, intimate displays such as the Houston Baseball Museum to major institutions like the Museum of Natural History and the Museum of Fine Arts, Houston's museums are as diversified as the people who visit and inhabit the City of Contrasts. Among the institutions cited here, at least several should catch the fancy of every reader—and add immeasurably to a memorable visit or a rediscovery of exciting and educational adventures in one's own backyard.

Bayou Bend Collection of the Museum of Fine Arts
1 Westcott Street
529-8773
The museum is housed in a 24-room colonial mansion, home of the late Miss Ima Hogg, daughter of former Texas Governor James Stephen Hogg. It includes a truly fine collection of American domestic arts and furnishings spanning 200 years from the Pilgrim era to early Victoriana.

Two-hour tours, limited to groups of four persons over the age of 16, are available by advance reservation

Since its formal dedication in 1966, Bayou Bend has been operated as a part of the Museum of Fine Arts.

Tuesday through Saturday mornings. (A small refundable deposit is required.) Children are welcome at Bayou Bend's open house from 1 to 5 on the second Sunday of each month. Closed during March and August.

Blaffer Gallery
Fine Arts Building—University of Houston Central Campus
4800 Calhoun
The Sarah Campbell Blaffer Gallery houses varied exhibits of local and international artists. Shows are changed periodically. Hours are 10 to 6 Tuesday through Saturday and 1 to 6 on Sunday. Closed Mondays, during the month of August, and on university holidays.

Burke Baker Planetarium is nestled between towering trees in Hermann Park.

Brazosport Museum of Natural History
101 This Way Street
Lake Jackson
265-7831

Located about 40 miles south of downtown Houston, the museum presents a wonderful exhibit of shells found on the Texas coast. Other displays include collections of coral, jade, and ivory. Open 10 to 5 Tuesdays through Sundays; closed on Monday.

Burke Baker Planetarium
1 Hermann Circle Drive (Hermann Park)
526-4273

This sophisticated planetarium and observatory features a modern optical telescope with a built-in television camera. Although there is a modest charge to view the sky programs, tours of the facilities and numerous scientific exhibits are offered free of charge. For additional information and reservations, call the planetarium office. The sky shows, presented three times each Saturday and Sunday, are changed five times a year. Call for specific times and charges. The planetarium is adjacent to the Museum of Natural Science.

Museums and Collections : 33

Contemporary Arts Museum
5216 Montrose
526-3129 or 526-6647
A wide variety of changing exhibits of paintings, sculptures, photographic prints, posters, and other media is housed in an ultramodern steel building. The museum tends to stress works by Texas artists. Exhibits have included creations by Calder, Buffet, Ernst, Matta, and others. Hours are 10 to 5 Tuesdays through Saturdays, and noon to 6 on Sundays.

Exhibits in the spacious rooms of the Contemporary Arts Museum are changed throughout the year.

Fort Bend County Museum
Houston Avenue at 5th Street
Richmond
342-6478
Texas historical artifacts, many dating back to the time of the state's original settlement, are displayed along with historic documents and photographs. On Sundays visitors can view the restored home of John M. Moore. Built about 1883, the structure is permanently situated on the museum grounds. Open 9 to 5 Tuesdays through Saturdays and 1 to 5 on Sundays.

Geophysical Society of Houston Museum
Geosource Building
6090 Southwest Freeway (I-59)
785-8898
Visitors can observe displays of instruments used in geophysical exploration dating back to the 1920s. Hours are 8 to 5 Mondays through Fridays.

Gulf Coast Railroad Museum
7390 Mesa
635-3255
Railway cars, including a mail, coach, observation, and sleeping car, all belonging to the Gulf Coast Chapter of the National Railway Historical Society, are open for public inspection on Sundays. A special treat for children and railroad buffs. Sunday hours are 11:30 to 4:30.

The Houston Baseball Museum
Finger's Furniture
Gulf Freeway (I-45 South) at Cullen
747-2443
The Houston Baseball Museum is centered around the last homeplate from old Buff Stadium, Houston's legendary former baseball park (predating Colt Stadium and the Astrodome). Located within a 14-acre furniture center, the museum houses baseball memorabilia of significance, much of which has been donated by the galaxy of

baseball stars who have visited it. Open 10:00 to 5:30 Monday through Saturday.

Houston Heritage Society
1100 Bagby (Sam Houston Park)
223-8367
This unusual collection of restored 19th-century buildings is located on the very edge of downtown Houston. The outdoor museum is on 20 acres of green grass and provides an architectural memento of Houston's frontier days. Although a guided tour of the buildings normally costs several dollars for adults (children's rates are very low), the grounds are open to the public without charge. During the Christmas season, free guided tours are given in the evening. For details, see the December listings in chapter 9. Eight restored structures are exhibited.

- **Kellum-Noble House.** Nathaniel Kellum, a transplanted Virginian who came to Houston to operate a brick kiln, built this elegant (for the time) two-story brick home in 1847. It may be the oldest brick house in Houston. One of the city's first private schools was operated in the structure during the 1850s by Mrs. Zerviah M. Noble.
- **The Long Row.** This 1967 reconstruction of Houston's first business building is a long wooden row of small stores and shops. The original structure, built in 1837 under the leadership of the Allen brothers, was destroyed by fire in 1860.
- **Nichols-Rice-Cherry House.** Saved from demolition and moved from its original site in 1897 by Mrs. E. Richardson Cherry, this Greek Revival–style home was originally constructed around 1850 by Ebenezer B. Nichols, a native of New York state. From 1851 to 1863, the home was owned by financier William Marsh Rice.
- **Pillot House.** Occupied by the Pillot family for nearly 100 years, this ornate, high Victorian–style home was built in 1868 by Eugene Pillot. The Heritage Society believes that this innovative home may have been the first in Houston to include an interior kitchen.
- **Sam Houston Park Bandstand.** A wide variety of free events takes place annually in this replica of the original bandstand, which dates back to the turn of the century. It is a well-known landmark of the city and, of course, of Sam Houston Park.

San Felipe Cottage (around 1870)

Pillot House (1868)

A reconstruction of the turn-of-the-century bandstand.

*St. John Church
(1891)*

*The Old Place
(around 1824)*

San Felipe Cottage. Typical of Texas cottages, circa 1870, this unadorned six-room home was originally built on the old San Felipe Road on the southwestern edge of the city.

St. John Church. This picturesque wooden country church was built in 1891 by the German agricultural community in northwestern Harris County. The original wooden pulpit and pews have been lovingly preserved by the Heritage Society.

The Old Place. The oldest permanent wooden structure in Harris County was built around 1824 using roughly cut cedar planks. Incorporated into a larger house by subsequent owners, the enlarged structure was once known as the Joseph Davis Plantation.

Houston Public Library
500 McKinney
224-5441
First-floor exhibits are changed monthly in the old Julia Ideson building. Next door in the new library building are changing exhibits from the library's permanent collection on the first floor and some upper rooms. Check at the main desk for further information. Hours are 9 A.M. to 9 P.M. Monday through Friday, 9 to 6 on Saturday, and 2 to 6 on Sunday.

Museum of American Architecture and Decorative Arts
Houston Baptist University Library, Second Floor
7502 Fondren Road
774-7661, ext. 311
Exhibits depict architecture and art from America's past. Four or five rotating shows per year include pre-Columbian African art, dolls of the world, and a large Christmas exhibit. Group tours can be arranged by appointment. The museum is open Tuesdays, Wednesdays, and Thursdays from 10 to 4 and on Sundays from 2 to 5.

Museum of Fine Arts
1001 Bissonnet
526-1361
The largest collection of fine arts in Houston is viewed by more than a quarter of a million visitors annually. The Finnigan collection displays objects of art from Egyptian, Greek, and Roman antiquity. The Kress and Straus collections feature paintings and bronze sculptures from the Renaissance. An impressive assortment of American Indian artwork native to the Southwest is complemented by a collection of Frederick Remington masterpieces. Other works from around the world and an often-changing Junior Gallery round out the art picture at this impressive institution. Architecturally noteworthy is the Brown Pavilion wing, which was designed by Mies Van der Rohe. Free guided tours are available with reser-

The Museum of Fine Arts has grown from the small building opened in 1924 to the nearly 150,000-square-foot superstructure that stands today.

vations Wednesday through Saturday at 1 P.M. and on Sunday at 2 P.M. There is truly something for everyone at the Museum of Fine Arts.

Hours are 10 to 5 Tuesday through Saturday and noon to 6 Sunday. Closed on Monday and major holidays.

Museum of Medical Science
5800 Caroline
529-3766
The Museum of Medical Science is a health museum dedicated to providing the public with information about the normal functions of the human body. Don't miss TAM, the Transparent Anatomical Manikin, who explains the various parts of her 5'8" body as each system lights up. (Special audio programs are available for youngsters

and Spanish-speaking visitors.) Other permanent exhibits cover basic physiology, dental care, drug abuse, and more. Height and weight scales can be used by the public. The museum also maintains some 75 portable exhibits that are made available to schools, paramedic groups, and other interested parties. Temporarily located on the second floor of the Museum of Natural Science, the Medical Science Museum will soon move to a new, greatly expanded facility at 1500 Hermann Drive.

Hours are 9:00 to 4:45 Tuesday through Saturday, and noon to 4:45 Sunday and Monday. Closed Thanksgiving, Christmas, and New Year's Days.

Museum of Natural Science
5800 Caroline
526-4273
Four generations of Houstonians have grown up with the Museum of Natural Science. Today the complex is one of the largest natural science museums in the Southwest. The 65-foot-long skeleton of a diplodocus, a herbivorous dinosaur, has found a home in the Main Level. Other exhibits cover space-age technology, geology (with large displays devoted to the formation, recovery, and processing of petroleum), archaeology, and natural history. The North and Central American Indian displays are particularly noteworthy. In all, the museum houses 90,000 square feet of exhibits, shows, study rooms, libraries, and lecture halls, as well as the Burke Baker Planetarium and (temporarily) the Museum of Medical Science. A particularly helpful staff can answer a good many surprisingly technical questions. Start at the information booth. The museum also conducts a large number of classes, film sessions, lectures, and other programs, some of which are free. Consult the information booth for word on these ever-changing events.

The museum is open Tuesday through Saturday from 9 to 5 (and again from 7:30 to 9:00 on Friday and Saturday evenings) and noon to 5 Sunday and Monday.

The past and present come face to face at the Museum of Natural Science.

Closed on Thanksgiving, Christmas, and New Year's Days.

O'Kane Gallery
University of Houston Downtown Campus—North Tower, Third Floor
1 Main Street
749-1950
Situated above Allen's Landing Park, the gallery is primarily devoted to works by artists from Houston and Texas. Many artists have had their first shows here, and there is always one interesting opening each month. The gallery is open Monday through Friday from 10 to 5 but is closed during the months of June, July, and August.

Pasadena Historical Museum
500 W. Jackson (Pasadena Memorial Park)
State Highway 225 at Shaver Exit
Pasadena
472-5812
Located near the San Jacinto Battleground, the museum depicts local history from simple pioneer days to today's

A small sculpture garden is adjacent to Rothko Chapel.

giant petrochemical plants. Exhibits include an early doctor's office and an old-fashioned kitchen. Normal hours are 1 to 5 Saturday and Sunday only, but special tours can be arranged for other days by calling 477-1511, ext. 450.

Rice University Museum
University Boulevard at Stockton
522-0866

Rotating exhibitions are sponsored by the Institute for the Arts. The museum is closed between exhibitions, so be sure to call ahead. Open 10 to 5 Tuesday through Saturday, noon to 6 Sunday. Closed on Monday.

Rothko Chapel
1409 Sul Ross Street
524-9839

Located just off West Alabama between the 1300 and 1400 blocks of Yupon, this octagonal chapel is home for 14 vast paintings by the late American abstract impressionist Mark Rothko. Printed information is available at the door. *The Broken Obelisk*, by Barnett Newman, a sculpture dedicated to the late Reverend Martin Luther King, Jr., is situated in a garden adjacent to the chapel. Open daily from 10 to 6.

Sam Houston Memorial Museum
Huntsville
295-7824
A scaled-down Greek Revival-style mansion, typical of East Texas homes from the 1840s, is across from Sam Houston State University, about a 1½-hour drive north of Houston on I-59. General Sam Houston lived in the home from 1848 to 1858. Open Tuesday through Sunday from 11 to 5.

San Jacinto Battleground
Highway 225 East
On April 21, 1836, the undermanned army of General Sam Houston routed the forces of Mexican General Santa Anna at this site in the decisive battle for Texas's independence. At various positions around the battlefield, the Daughters of the Republic of Texas have placed historic markers to commemorate campsites, advances, and other significant events in the 18-minute battle that opened the way for U.S. expansion to the Pacific. Maps showing the locations of the markers can be obtained from the San Jacinto Monument and Museum.

Nestled between the San Jacinto River and Buffalo Bayou, portions of the battlefield have always been marshy. Recently, however, extensive industrial tapping of underground water at the site has caused considerable damage to some parts of the park. The grounds are open daily from 10 to 6.

San Jacinto Monument and Museum of Texas History
San Jacinto Battleground (State Highway 225 East)
479-2421
The 570-foot monument—the tallest monumental column in the world—weighs more than 70 million pounds and is topped by a lone star that is 35 feet across and weighs 22

The towering monument at San Jacinto Battleground is taller than the Washington Monument.

Only an exterior view of the U.S.S Texas is free.

tons! The monument commemorates the heroes of the Texas War for Independence with eight massive panels, including a frieze and an account of the famous battle. The museum housed in the monument's base recalls the history of the region from the times of the Indians who greeted Cortez to Texas statehood. The museum and monument can be entered without cost, but there is a fee to ride the elevator to the top.

Monday through Saturday hours are 9:30 to 5:30 (10:00 to 5:30 on Sunday). Closed Christmas Day.

U.S.S. *Texas* Battleship
3527 Battleground Road
LaPorte
479-2411
The grand veteran of two world wars and a dozen campaigns is permanently moored at the San Jacinto Battleground. Although visitors will need to pay a fee to board the ship and enter the five museums devoted to Texas and U.S. naval power aboard her, landlubbers can view the ship's impressive exterior without cost. Hours are 10 to 7 from May to Labor Day; 11 to 5 the rest of the year.

CHAPTER 4

Houston parks and recreation

Houston has 250-plus municipal parks that cover more than 7,500 land acres and nearly twice that much acreage of water. At various locations within the system are five 18-hole golf courses (*not* free of charge), more than 40 free swimming pools, a total of 112 free neighborhood tennis courts (three additional tennis centers charge for court time), more than 200 baseball fields, a dozen soccer and rugby fields, and more than 50 community recreation centers that offer a variety of free classes and courses. We will discuss some of these free recreational opportunities later in this chapter.

Some especially noteworthy parks in the city are: Hermann Park, with its zoo, natural science museum, planetarium, and garden center; Memorial Park, featuring an arboretum, herb gardens, botanical hall, and three-mile parcours jogging trail; and Eisenhower Park on the San Jacinto River below the Lake Houston Dam, offering nature studies and good fishing. Park development in downtown Houston includes Tranquility Park in the Civic Center, the expansion of Allen's Landing Park at Main and Commerce, and the transformation of Buffalo Bayou into an expansive area for outdoor activities such as jogging and bicycling. The newest of Houston's

A duck pond adjacent to the Hermann Park Zoo is maintained by the Houston Parks and Recreation Dept.

major parks is Herman Brown Park, opened on the near east side on November 1, 1980.

Harris County maintains 58 parks covering almost 7,000 total acres. Major parks include Armand Bayou Nature Center, a wilderness preserve with nature trails and scenic boat tours on Armand Bayou; Sylvan Beach, a popular boating and fishing area near LaPorte; Clear Lake Park, with boating and fishing on Clear Lake; Alexander Deussen Park, offering boating, fishing, and camping on Lake Houston; and Bear Creek Park, with picnicking facilities on Addicks Reservoir land. Many of these areas are described elsewhere in this book, so the ones enumerated here will focus on Houston proper and those peripheral spots we missed.

Allen's Landing
Main and Commerce (downtown)
The site of Houston's birth is named for A.C. and J.K.

48 : 500 THINGS TO DO IN HOUSTON FOR FREE

A number of changes are in the works for Allen's Landing, the site of Houston's birth.

Allen. A good spot for walking and viewing the Houston skyline, the park is open daily.

Allen Parkway Recreation Area
Bounded by Allen Parkway and Sabine, Shepherd, and Memorial drives
This expansive area just west of the downtown district is the ideal place to view the city's skyline while walking, jogging, or bicycling. There are picnic areas and benches all along the winding trails that lead visitors

across wooden bridges and past rolling hills that rise above historic Buffalo Bayou. Open daily.

Herman Brown Park
455 Oates (on the near east side)
The city's first "parkwarming" was held on November 1, 1980, opening this 842-acre site, which is being completed in stages. Phase I improvements include tennis courts, a basketball court, softball fields, and a million-dollar recreational center. About 75 percent of the park is wooded with pines and mixed hardwoods. Picnic tables and barbecue cookers have been installed as has a hike-and-bike trail. Open daily.

Sam Houston Park
Allen Parkway at Bagby
A grassy island on the edge of downtown Houston, this park is the home of a number of historic buildings restored by the Houston Heritage Society. (See Houston Heritage Society in chapter 3.) The *Angel of the Confederacy* statue is situated along the banks of a small lagoon in the shadow of major expressways towering overhead.

Memorial Park
Memorial Drive at I-610 (West Loop)
In addition to its arboretum, botanical gardens, golf course, and tennis center (golf and tennis are not free), the park boasts one of the finest parcours exertrails in the Southwest. The scenery is beautiful.

Hermann Park
Main Street, south of downtown
Houston's major central park contains the zoo, Miller Theater, Museum of Natural Science, Burke-Baker Planetarium, the Houston Garden Center, and a new jogging course that winds past the International Pagoda. Playgrounds and picnic areas are abundant.

50 : 500 THINGS TO DO IN HOUSTON FOR FREE

Symbolic rockets are dwarfed by downtown skyscrapers in Tranquility Park, one of a number of sites providing a home to the Houston Festival held each March.

Tranquility Park
Bounded by Smith, Rusk, Bagby, and Walker streets
Commemorating NASA's Apollo flights, especially Apollo XI, the park features a two-block, 32-level fountain with five towers resembling rockets.

OUTDOOR RECREATION

Because of Houston's year-round semitropical climate, the outdoors are available for play and exercise most days of the year. Visitors as well as residents are invited to take advantage of all the facilities in the city's extensive park and recreation acreage.

Exertrails
Resembling outdoor obstacle courses, exertrails provide systematic exercise for all the muscles in participants' bodies. Exercisers run, jog, or walk to various stations at which printed instructions describe correct exercising techniques. There are four such trails in Houston, but the two most popular are in Hermann and Memorial parks.

The Hermann Park trail is just under two miles long. It begins at the Garden Center, continues west behind the Hermann Regional Center, follows the perimeter of the golf course south, and then turns back north toward the Garden Center, just off Golf Course Drive. The Memorial Park Exertrail is a three-mile loop that begins west of the tennis center and continues southward by Memorial

Joggers keep in shape along an exertrail in Hermann Park. Plans call for evenutally joining all city paths to form a 31-mile marathon trail.

Loop Drive to Memorial Drive, returning to the tennis center on the north side of Memorial Loop Drive. Other exertrails are located in MacGregor and Brays Bayou parks. For more information, call 641-4111.

Bicycle Trails

Bicycle trails in Houston's parks have been lengthened considerably in recent years. Of the three types of bikeways established by the Parks and Recreation Department, those designated as bike trails (and indicated by broad dotted lines on the official city maps reproduced on these pages) are probably the safest and most satisfying since they are away from automobile traffic.

Houston Parks and Recreation : 53

HOUSTONS HIKE & BIKEWAYS

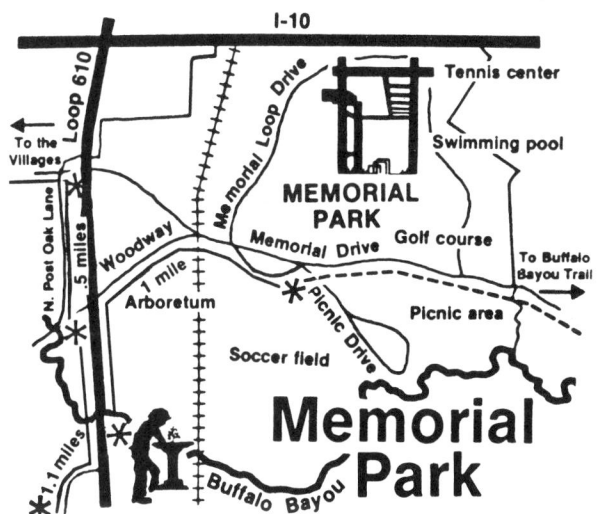

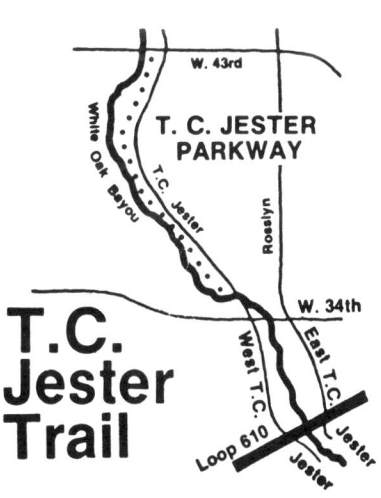

T.C. Jester Trail

·········· **HIKE AND BIKE TRAIL:** a path separated from roadways — motor vehicles not allowed.

────── **HIKE AND BIKE ROUTE:** roadway signed for bicycle travel as well as all other types of traffic.

- - - - - - - - **PROPOSED TRAIL:** paths to be built in the future.

OCTOBER 1980,   Subject to revision

All bikeways maps are courtesy of Houston Parks and Recreation Dept.

54 : 500 THINGS TO DO IN HOUSTON FOR FREE

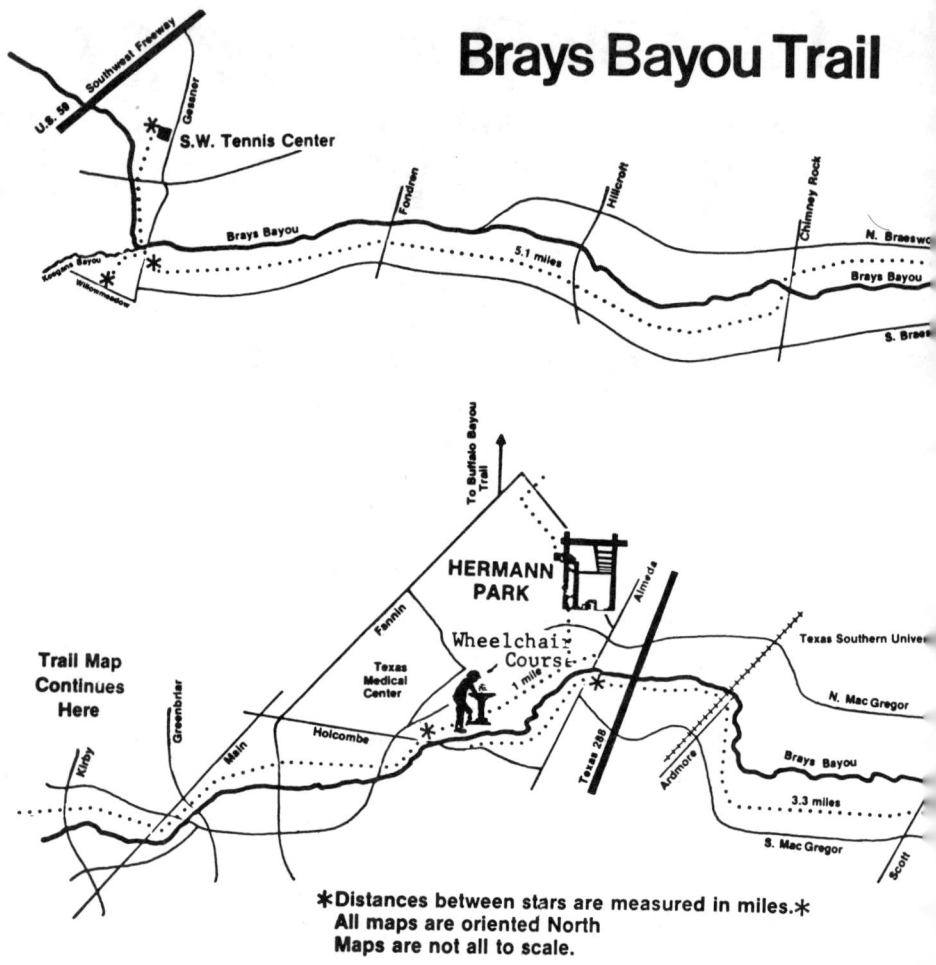

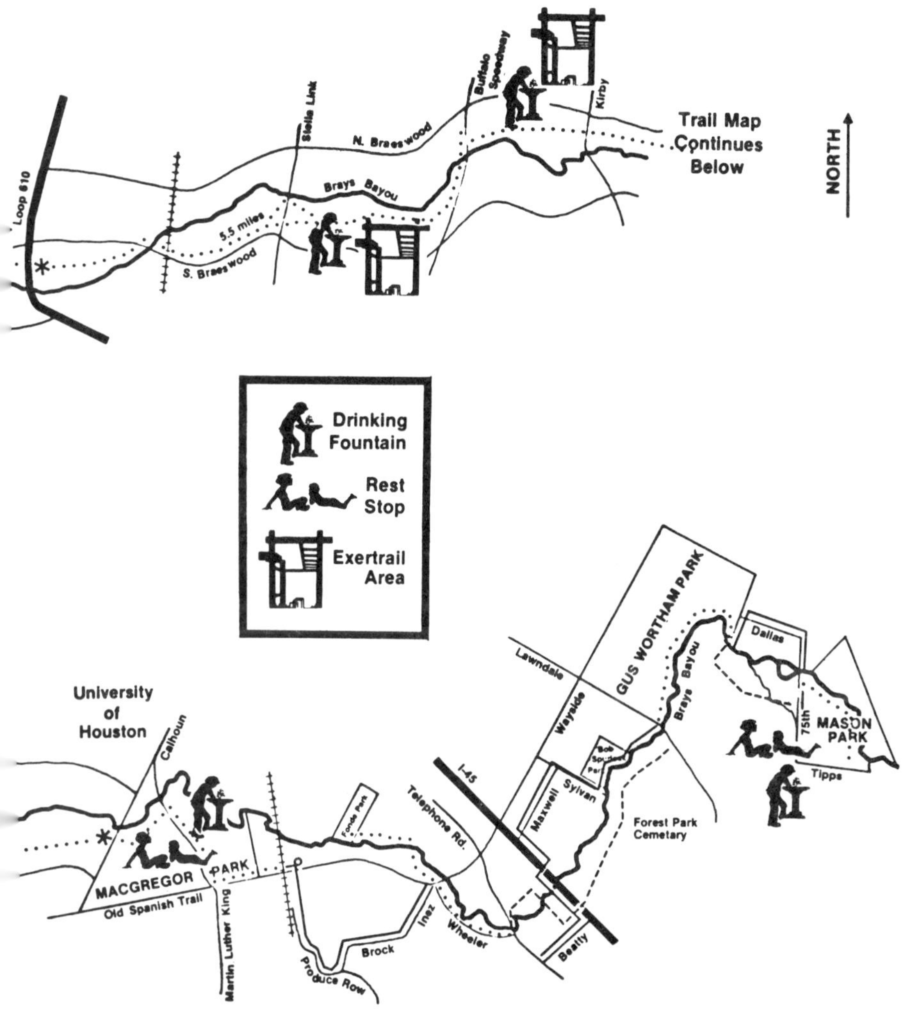

Houston Parks and Recreation : 55

Buffalo Bayou Trail

Outdoor Gymnasiums and Basketball Shelters

All of the sport pavilions listed are outdoors and lighted for night use. Most of the sites have accompanying playgrounds.

Charlton Park (SE)
8200 Park Place Blvd.
645-3589

Clark Park (N)
200 Dipping Lane

Clinton Park (SE)
200 Mississippi
673-0955

Cloverland Park (S)
11800 Scott
733-4581

Crestmont Park (SE)
5200 Selinsky
733-2236

DeZavalla Park (SE)
7521 Avenue H
923-5163

Dodson Lake Park (NE)
9010 Dodson
692-4573

Garden Villas Park (SE)
6720 South Haywood
649-5460

Godwin Park (SW)
5101 Rutherglen
729-9850

Hobart Taylor Park (NE)
8100 Kenton
674-3959

Independence Heights Park (NW)
603 East 35th
861-8503

Ingrando Park (SE)
7302 Keller
643-4764

Lakewood Park (NE)
8811 Feland
631-2780

Lincoln Park (N)
979 Greenshaw
447-0158

Linkwood Park (SW)
3699 Norris
664-9851

MacGregor Park (SE)
5225 Calhoun
747-8650

Proctor Plaza Park (NW)
803 West Temple
862-6907

Settegast Park (Central)
3000 Garrow
224-2798

Shady Lane Park (N)
10220 Shady Lane

Sunnyside Park (E)
3502 Bellfort
734-5061

Swiney Park (NE)
2812 Cline
223-2094

Windsor Village (SW)
14441 Croquet
729-4260

A gymnastics class at the Hermann Regional Center.

INDOOR RECREATION CENTERS AND GYMNASIUMS

The Houston Parks and Recreation Department operates a baker's dozen recreation centers that offer indoor gymnasium facilities and a wide assortment of classes in physical fitness, arts, and crafts. (Nearly three dozen also offer a variety of classes. For the names and locations of those nearest you, call 520-7014.) All of the centers have full-size basketball courts and some have racquetball courts. General information about the gym facilities and hours can be obtained by calling 641-4111. For additional data about specific centers near you, call the local centers at the numbers listed at the end of this section.

Classes for the General Public

The Parks and Recreation Department regularly schedules classes led by qualified instructors in aerobic exercise, arts and crafts, dance, dancercise, drama, gymnastics, judo, karate, playschool, square dancing, and weight lifting. Most of the courses are entirely free, but a few charge nominal fees for materials and equipment use. For information on specific classes, hours, and locations, call 520-7014.

Therapeutic Recreation
For information about special classes for the deaf, blind,

A martial arts class at the Godwin Park Recreational Center.

60 : 500 THINGS TO DO IN HOUSTON FOR FREE

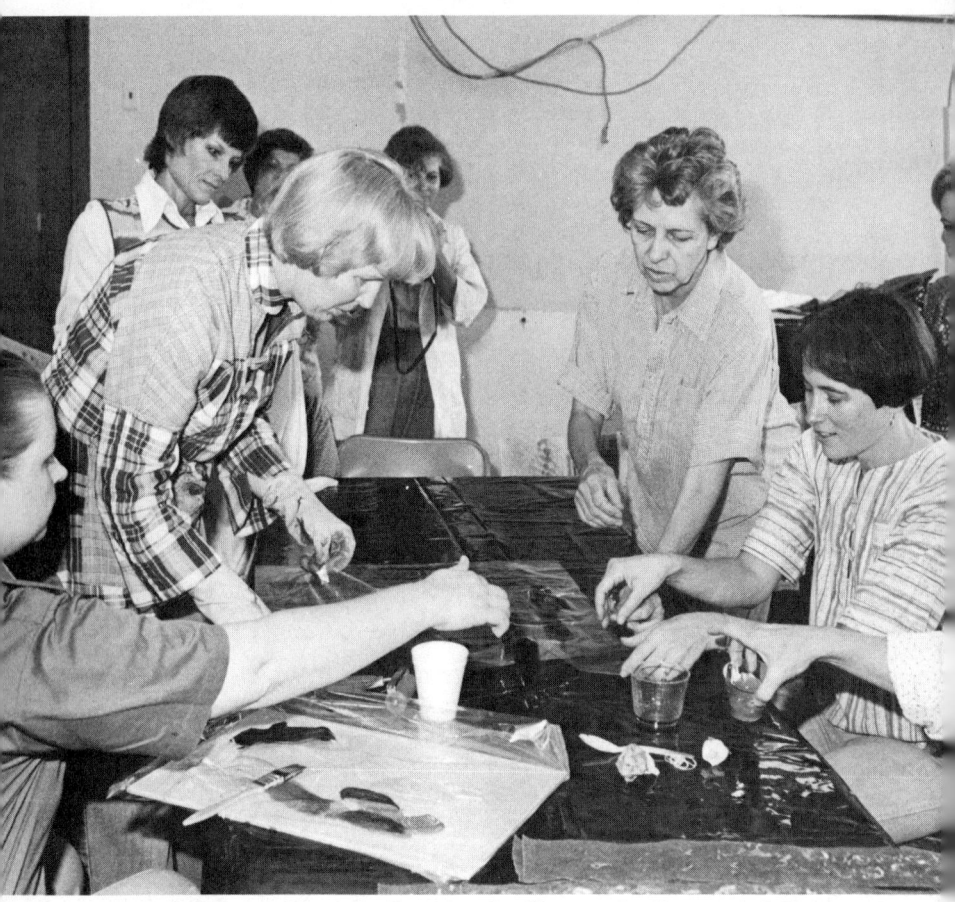

A fabric dyeing class at the Hermann Regional Center.

developmentally disabled, and occupationally handicapped, call 641-4111, ext. 512.

Senior Citizen Classes
Free programs prepared specifically for senior citizens include arts and crafts, bridge, games, dancing, painting, sewing, and singing. Get the details by calling 641-4111, ext. 503.

Recreation Center Locations

Here are 13 locations where it all happens!

Candlelight Park (NW)
1520 Candlelight
682-3587

Denver Harbor (NE)
6400 Market
675-2151

Edgewood Park (SE)
5803 Bellfort
734-8434

**Emancipation Park
(S Central)**
3018 Dowling
528-2500

Finnegan Park (NE)
4900 Providence
674-9220

Hartman Park (SE)
9311 East Avenue P
921-0106

Hermann Park (Central)
2020 Hermann Drive
222-5525

Highland Park (NW)
3316 DeSoto
683-6960

Love Park (NW)
1000 West 12th
861-6336

Mason Park
541 South 75th
928-2118

Moody Park (NW)
3725 Fulton
694-3554

Stude Park (NW)
1031 Stude
869-3154

Woodland Park
212 Parkview
862-1687

Some Parks and Recreation Department classes are taught in other locations. For details call 520-7014.

SWIMMING POOLS

More than 40 free pools are open to the public during the summer, generally from early May through Labor Day. Monday through Saturday hours are 10 A.M. to 1 P.M., 2 P.M. to 5 P.M., and 6 P.M. to 8 P.M. Sunday hours are from 6 P.M. to 8 P.M.

Swimmers escape the summer heat at Westbury Pool.

Beverly Hills
9800 Kingsport

Clinton
203 Mississippi

Cloverland
3800 Hickok

Denver Harbor
1020 Gazin

DeZavalla
7521 Avenue H

Dodson Lake
9010 Dodson

Dunlavy
4400 Dunlavy

Eastwood
5000 Harrisburg

Emancipation
3018 Dowling

Finnigan
4900 Providence

Glenbrook
8201 North Bayou Drive

Grady
1700 Yorktown

Greenwood
602 Beresford

Hermann
2020 Hermann Drive

Hester House
2020 Solo

Independence House
603 East 35th Street

Lansdale
8201 Roos Road

Lawrence
725 Lawrence

Levy
3000 Richmond

Lincoln
1048 Crenshaw

Love
1000 West 12th

MacGregor
5225 Calhoun

Mason
75th and Tipps

Memorial
6402 Arnot

Moody
3201 Fulton

Moses Leroy
3000 Trulley

Northline
6911 Nordling

Oak Forest
1400 Dubarry

Reveille
7700 Oak Vista

Schwartz
8203 Vogue

Settegast
3000 Garrow

Springwood
Hammerly and West Belt

Stude
1031 Stude

Sunnyside 3502 Bellfort	**Tuffly** Russell and Lucille	**Wilson** 100 Gilpin
T.C. Jester 4205 T.C. Jester	**Westbury** 10605 Mullins	**Yellowstone** 6900 LaSallette
Townwood 3403 Simsbrook	**Wiley** Gillette and Ruthven	

In June and July, free swimming classes are conducted at a number of locations by the American Red Cross. Generally, participants must be at least six years old, but younger children may be accepted if they have at least beginning swimming skills. Call 641-4111 for details.

NEIGHBORHOOD TENNIS COURTS

Adhering strictly to the freebie spirit of this book, we will not list the three enormous tennis centers operated by the Parks and Recreation Department since all charge a use fee. But tennis enthusiasts can find love, victory, and all points in between at a total of 82 courts at 41 different locations that are operated entirely free of charge in the various neighborhood parks. They can also find free tennis lessons by calling 641-4111. Classes are available for children and adults, but participants must supply their own rackets.

PARK	LOCATION	COURTS
Anderson (SW)	Schumacher and Bering	2 Lighted
Beverly Hills (SE)	Kingspoint and Fonville	1 Unlighted
Cherryhurst (W Central)	Cherryhurst and Windsor	1 Lighted
Charlton (SE)	Park Place and River Dr.	2 Lighted
Chimney Rock (SW)	11655 Chimney Rock	3 Lighted
Denver Harbor (E)	Market and Henke	2 Lighted
Dodson Lake (NE)	Dodson and Laura Koppe	2 Lighted
Dow #1 (SE)	Rockhill and Wilmerdean	2 Lighted
Dunlavy (SW)	Dunlavy and S/W Fwy.	1 Unlighted
Eastwood (E)	Harrisburg and Dumble	1 Unlighted
Emancipation (SE)	Elgin and Dowling	2 Lighted
Finnigan (E)	Sonora and Callis	2 Lighted
Fleming (SW)	Sunset and Kent	2 Unlighted

64 : 500 THINGS TO DO IN HOUSTON FOR FREE

PARK	LOCATION	COURTS
Freeway Manor (SE)	Theta and Bronson	1 Lighted
Grady (SW)	San Felipe and Yorktown	1 Lighted
Graham (NW)	540 W. 34th	1 Lighted
Greenwood (E)	Beresford and Halifax	2 Lighted
Hermann (S)	Holcombe and Fannin	4 Lighted
Highland (NW)	DeSoto	2 Unlighted
Ingrando (SE)	Keller and Coral	2 Lighted
Jaycee (W Central)	Seamist and Grovewood	1 Lighted
Jones (SE)	Coastway and Gulfdale	2 Lighted
Karl Young (SW)	Stella Link and Tartan	1 Unlighted
Law (SE)	Mykawa and Vassar	2 Unlighted
Lincoln (N)	Grenshaw and Arabela	1 Unlighted
Linkwood (SW)	Ilona and Norris	2 Lighted
Mangum Manor (NW)	Costa Rica and Saxon	1 Unlighted
Mason (SE)	75th and Tipps	4 Lighted
Meadowcreek (SE)	Forest Oaks and Berry Ck.	2 Lighted
Memorial (NW)	Ford and Haskell	4 Unlighted
Meyerland (SW)	Prichett and Jason	2 Lighted
Milroy (W Central)	Yale and 12th	1 Lighted
Montie Beach (W Central)	Coronado and Northwood	2 Lighted
Moody (N)	3800 Fulton	2 Lighted
Northline (N)	Nording and Twickenham	2 Lighted
Oak Forest (NW)	Oak Forest and DuBarry Ln.	2 Lighted
Proctor Plaza (W Central)	W. Temple and Watson	1 Lighted
River Oaks (W Central)	Larchmont and Locke Ln.	4 Unlighted
Scenic Woods (NE)	Gleason and Cheeves	2 Lighted
Sharpstown (SW)	Braes Acres and Carew	2 Lighted
Westwood (SW)	4044 Leemac	2 Lighted
Willow (SW)	Waynesboro and Cliffwood	2 Lighted
Woodland (N)	Houston and Parkview	2 Lighted

The Houston Sleeper

No discussion of Houston's parks would be complete without a mention of Martha Hermann Square. Located at the intersection of Smith and Bagby, this park surrounds the City Hall reflection pool. It was donated to the city by George Hermann (Hermann Park) with the stipulations that it should be named after his mother and that anyone who wanted to sleep undisturbed by the forces of law and order could use the park for that purpose.

CHAPTER 5

special places

Houston is fairly bursting with a Texas-sized assortment of fascinating places that are as enjoyable to visit as they are difficult to categorize. A reminder of the city's past is served up in a cornucopia of historic churches, buildings, and even entire districts, more than a few of which are in now decaying neighborhoods, standing virtually side by side with nude bars and dilapidated buildings.

The city has become one of today's leading centers of commerce and industry, and a number of its business concerns offer free guided tours of these commercial centers. Some of the finest—and, of course, largest—shopping centers anywhere are right here, fine places for window shopping during those summer heat waves. The Fabulous 50 Miles of the Port of Houston stretches out along both sides of the Houston Ship Channel, beckoning sight-seers to a free observation platform to watch activity in the nation's third-busiest port. Here, too, is where visitors can enjoy a free ride on the port's inspection boat, the *Sam Houston.*

For a glimpse into the future, the LBJ Space Center offers the widest variety of tours, talks, and films this side of the Milky Way to anyone interested in learning more about the final frontier. With fewer facilities for public inspection, the fast-growing and already enormous Medical Center complex in central Houston is a place for self-directed touring in a relaxing parklike atmosphere.

American Red Cross—Harris County Chapter
Kirby Drive at Southwest Freeway
526-8300 (ask for Safety Programs)
Free courses in First Aid, CPR (cardiopulmonary resuscitation), Small Craft Safety, Lifesaving, and Home Nursing Care are offered throughout the year. Call ahead for details.

Anheuser-Busch
775 Gellhorn
675-2311
See the brewing process and objects of the art of brewing during a guided tour that ends with an invitation to the reception area for a free sampling of Anheuser-Busch products. Hours are 10:00 to 4:30 Monday through Saturday and noon to 6 on Sunday.

Annunciation Church
600 Crawford
The stone edifice is a fine example of Romanesque Revival architecture. At times, early morning and late afternoon sunlight sifting through the stained-glass windows in the beautiful tower gives the church the appearance of an inner glow.

Antioch Baptist Church
313 Robin
Located just behind Allen Center, this church played a significant role in the black history of the area. It is the oldest black church in Houston and appears on the National Register of Historic Places. Open daily.

The tower of Annunciation Church rises above a somewhat decaying neighborhood.

Barker's Dam Telescope Tour
South of I-10 at Addicks exit
The Burke-Baker Planetarium sponsors an unusual astronomic event on each clear Friday night (most often from May to August) at 9 P.M. After a brief lecture describing the nighttime sky as it appears during the current season, planets are identified and then viewed through six high-power telescopes set up at the top of the dam. After each person has viewed the planets, the telescopes are readjusted to study other celestial formations. The tours are conducted at the south end of the parking lot. To reach the dam, take I-10 to the Addicks exist and drive south for one mile on State Highway 6. For additional information, call the Burke-Baker Planetarium at 526-4273.

CEMETERIES

A unique way to learn about the history of Houston is to visit some of its larger cemeteries. This small section of our book is designed for the history buff and the curious or for anyone who enjoys the serenity and natural beauty that can so often be found on cemetery grounds.

Glenwood Cemetery, 2609 Washington. Howard Hughes is buried here, along with many of the developers of the early Texas Republic as well as Houston. Reading the historic names on tombstones here is like listening to a rollcall of Houston streets. The keeper's cottage is a fine example of Victorian architecture.

Hollywood Cemetery, North Main at Houston Avenue. Many 19th-century graves tell much of Houston's past in this beautiful and peaceful setting. The grounds include extensive acreage along the banks of Little White Oak Bayou.

Magnolia Cemetery, Montrose Boulevard between Allen Parkway and West Dallas. Houston's Chicano heritage is much in evidence in this island of tranquility deep in the thick of the city's hustle and bustle.

St. Vincents Cemetery, Navigation and St. Charles streets. Dick Dowling, the hero of the Civil War's Battle of Sabina, is buried here, along with Samuel Paschal, hero of the Battle of San Jacinto.

Washington Cemetery, 2911 Washington. Here rests Emma Seely, combat veteran of the Civil War and author of a best-selling book from the 1870s entitled *The Nurse and the Spy.* Some very old headstones can be viewed among the trees.

Houston Pet Cemetery, 2640 Fountainview, and **Special Pals Petland,** 4211 Bellaire. Here are two final resting places for man's special friends.

Christ Church Cathedral
1117 Texas Avenue
222-2593

Founded in 1839, Houston's oldest church still on its original site is a splendid example of Medieval Gothic architecture. The church is overgrown with ivy brought from Westminster Abbey around 1880. Art objects include at least one stained-glass window by Tiffany, handcarved woodwork, and statuary. The office is open on weekdays from 8 to 5. If asked politely, the staff will open the cathedral for interested visitors.

Coca-Cola Bottling Plant
669-3106
Visitors can watch the highly automated bottling process of the world's most famous soft drink. The company requests that visitors call ahead for tour reservations and directions to the tour site. Tours are conducted Monday through Friday at 10:00 and 1:30. Groups of up to 200 can be accommodated, but it is best to make reservations two to four weeks ahead.

Crispin Building
Caroline at Texas
Completed in 1922 as a Branch Federal Reserve Bank, the original untouched lobby now displays a 12-foot model of the ship *Bohemian*.

Farmers Market Cooperative
2520 Airline (off 610 Loop North)
Large and small shipments of fresh fruits and vegetables are brought in daily. Produce can be purchased in huge lots or by the pound. It's fun to watch the vegetable action, which is particularly frantic in the early morning. Open Monday through Saturday.

Galleria
5015 Westheimer
621-7251
This magnificent three-level enclosed shopping mall, built around an Olympic-sized skating rink beneath a glass-domed skylight, is a unique modern concept based on the Galleria of Milan, Italy, built in 1860 by Vittoria Emanuele.

Skaters are warmed by the light of the sun on the ice rink in the Galleria.

Phase I, completed in 1970, and Phase II, completed in 1977, now encompass more than a million square feet of shopping space. Internationally known department stores, hotels, boutiques, and appealing restaurants add flavor to the magic of this monument to commercialism. As fascinating as a walk through any museum, a hefty dose of marketing resistance will net the visitor an unparalleled free afternoon's delight. The mall is open from 10 to 9 Monday through Saturday. It is also open for the same hours on Sunday, when all the stores are closed.

Goodwill Industries
5200 Jensen
692-6221
Goodwill Industries of Houston offers free tours of its 22-acre rehabilitation center for handicapped persons. The center includes a dental clinic, greenhouse, and computer programming and clerical skills classrooms. Open Monday through Friday from 9:30 A.M. to 3:30 P.M.

Albert Thomas Center builders saved the Hanging Tree from a death sentence when they redesigned the convention center around it.

The Hanging Tree
Capitol and Bagby (next to Albert Thomas Center)
Believed to be more than 400 years old, this large oak is probably the oldest tree in Harris County. Diaries from the 1800s have been found written by people who expected to die on the Hanging Tree, but nothing has ever been proved. Adding to the speculation is the fact that the tree is quite close to the old county court building.

Hilltop Herb Farm
P.O. Box 866
Cleveland
1-592-5859
Each weekend, this privately owned herb farm is open for public inspection. The gardens contain more than 1,500 varieties of herbs. Lunch and dinner (which, alas, are not free) are available by reservation at the well-known restaurant located on the farm.

Houston Fire Department, Station Number 1
410 Bagby
222-5561
See equipment, fire trucks, fire fighters, and daily procedures at an authentic working fire station. Call for reservations well in advance of the date you plan to visit.

Imperial Sugar
U.S. Highway 59 South
491-9181, ext. 268
The Imperial Sugar refinery is just a few miles southwest of Houston on Highway 59. Visitors to the facility can view the entire process by which raw cane sugar is refined, packaged, and brought to supermarket shelves. The tour lasts about one hour, and comfortable shoes and dress are recommended. Tours begin at 10 A.M. and 2 P.M. Monday through Friday. Although reservations are not always necessary, it's best to call ahead.

Kennedy Trading Post (now known as La Carafe)
813 Congress on Old Market Square
Erected as a trading post for the Alabama and Lipan Indians, this is Houston's oldest commercial building still on its original site. Many Houstonians now visit the structure to trade the current coin of the realm for alcoholic beverages. A collection of historic photographs lines the interior walls. The building is listed in the National Register of Historic Places.

Houston Underground Tunnel System
Various downtown locations
Maintained for pedestrian travel in the heart of the downtown business district, this network of interconnected tunnels provides an occasional glimpse into the workings of the giant buildings above as well as a look into the security of a major bank. The system can be entered from the lowest level of these buildings: Shell Plaza, Houston Center, Entex, Tenneco, 1 Allen Center, Gulf Buildings.

The oldest commercial building in Houston, now known as La Carafe, is located in Old Market Square, the city's gaslight district.

HISTORIC DOWNTOWN BUILDINGS

From New York to Chicago to Los Angeles and back again through Houston, Atlanta, and Miami, the debate rages on. As every major American city comes of age, special-interest groups and power brokers line up on one side of the issue or the other. To some, the past is as important a link to the identity of a great city as the future, with historic landmarks providing one of the few tangible ingredients in an ever shorter recipe of metropolitan heritage. Historic buildings are viewed as islands of history and charm in an age of angular steel and glass. Others view these very same buildings as dirty old firetraps, expensive to heat and cool, inefficient in their use of space, nearly impossible to clean, and often downright eyesores, candidates for the first available wrecking ball as the wheel of progress inevitably turns.

Downtown Houston has more than two dozen buildings worthy of historic note. Unless you are a student of architecture, few are worth a special trip to the inner city to see, but most deserve at least a passing glance when you are downtown.

In the list of historic buildings that follows, almost all of the information was taken from materials prepared and furnished by Frances Lawrence of the Harris County Heritage Society. All the buildings on the list are generally inside the boundaries formed by Louisiana, Texas, Fannin, and Commerce streets and are more or less presented in an order progressing from Louisiana to Fannin.

Alley Theater Building, 615 Texas (around the corner from Louisiana); 1969—Ulrich, Franzen, Mackie, & Kamrath. Headquarters for the famous theater troupe.

Brashear Building, 401–3 Travis; 1868; Isaac Brashear was a state senator. He and his son John (a county judge) built the building on land purchased in 1839. Next door, at 405–7 Travis, is the Simmler Building, also built in 1868.

Atlanta Life Insurance Company (the Bowery), Louisiana at Prairie. This is the headquarters of the oldest black life insurance company in Texas.

Hogg Building, 410 Louisiana; 1920–1—Barglebaugh and Whitson. The Hogg Building was financed by Will and Mike Hogg. Originally it housed the Armour Ford Co. The elegant penthouse at top was occupied by the Hogg brothers and was surrounded by a rooftop lawn, exotic plants, and fountains imported from Italy.

Roco Building, 419 Travis (at Prairie); 1870. The structure originally housed a meat market. The original canopy over the sidewalk remains.

Hermann Building (Salvation Army), 204 Travis; 1917. Built by the George Hermann estate, construction was originally started without a building permit.

Old Cotton Exchange Building, 202 Travis; 1884—Eugene Heiner. Note the exchange floor and the restored murals in this Renaissance Revival–style edifice made from red Philadelphia pressed brick and stone.

Southern Pacific Building, Travis and Franklin; 1910—Jarvis Hunt & Co. When constructed, this was the largest office building created to house a single company's employees. It had an innovative ice-water refrigeration system for air conditioning.

Magnolia Brewery, 719 Franklin; 1896—remodeled in 1915 by H.C. Cook. Leaded-glass windows highlight magnolia blossom. The building served as the tap room for the brewery.

W.L. Foley Building, 214–6 Travis; 1889—Eugene Heiner. Although the first floors of almost all historic buildings in Houston have been destroyed, this one is intact! W.L. was related to the famous Foleys of today but was notoriously cheap. Note the roofline along the Travis block that W.L. refused to spend the money to even out.

Kennedy Corner (Keith Hotel), 220 Travis; 1889. Site of the Kennedy trading post, which suffered fire damage.

Kennedy Bakery (La Carafe), 813 Congress; 1860s—architect unknown. The bakery served the trading post next door.

Henry Brashear Building, 910 Prairie; 1888—Eugene Heiner. The entire structure was built by a son of Isaac Brashear for the exorbitant sum of $8,500.

Si Packer's Troy Laundry (the Shoe Market), 912 Prairie; Si Packer introduced steam laundry to Texas in 1890. In its heyday, the laundry finished 1,000 shirts daily. A total of 41 workers (excluding delivery truck drivers) were employed.

Dickson Building, 800 Commerce; 1905. Now occupied by law offices, the edifice is actually two buildings with a party wall.

Rice Hotel, Main and Texas; 1912—Mauran, Russell, and Crowell. For many decades, this was the site of the largest and finest hotel in Houston. Also the site of the first state capitol. The building has been vacant and boarded up for several years, but it was sold recently. Its future is in grave jeopardy.

Christ Church Cathedral, Fannin and Texas; 1893—Silas McBee. The home of the oldest church congregation in Houston is discussed at greater length earlier in this chapter.

Civil Courts Building, Fannin and Congress; 1911—Wang and Witchell. The edifice is a perfect example of the Beaux Arts style of architecture.

B.A. Shepherd Building, 219 Main; 1883—George Dickey. The building was surrounded by a two-story iron canopy, which was removed many years ago to reveal interesting architectural details. The Houston National Bank was headquartered here from 1889 to 1912.

South Texas National Bank, 215 Main; 1910—C.D. Hill (William Ward Watkins added the two wings in 1922). The structure originally had two double bronze doors and a 45-foot atrium that was closed up in 1961. The building was sold recently and will probably be used for office space.

Pan American Building, Main and Congress; 1911—Mauran, Russell, and Crowell. The arched openings exhibit keystones with female figures. At present the entire building is vacant except for the ground floors.

Commercial National Bank, 917 Franklin; 1905—Green and Swarz. Note the remaining balustrade; many were blown off in storms over the years. The side entrance is original.

Dorrance Building (Travelers Hotel), 112-4 Main; 1903—Green and Swarz. The top floor was added later with little consideration of the building beneath it. The first floor was originally cast iron.

Merchants and Manufacturers Building (University of Houston Downtown Campus), Main and Buffalo Bayou; 1929—Gisikey and Harris. Based on Chicago's Merchandise Mart, this was the largest building in Houston at the time of its construction.

Scanlon Building, 405 Main; 1910—Daniel Burnham (a well-known Chicago architect). In its era this was the tallest building in Houston.

Pillot Building, 1016 Congress; 1860. One of the oldest iron-front structures in the city, it has been vacant since 1977 and is in danger of condemnation. The owner, Harris County, refuses to restore it.

Sweeney, Coombs, and Fredericks, 301 Main; 1889. This Victorian building was recently restored by Harris County at a cost of $130,000 (far more than the original cost of construction).

Kiam Building, Main and Preston; 1893—Holland, Dickey, and Lorehn. The building featured the first electric elevator in Houston (the nation's third). The innovative structure had more than five miles of electrical wiring.

Intercontinental Airport
Off I-45 North or U.S. 59 North
433-4395

Free guided tours of this major aviation facility for groups of ten or more can be arranged by calling the airport at least 24 hours in advance of the date you wish to attend. Of course, smaller groups can just go to the airport and "hangar around," watching takeoffs and landings and walking through the enormous terminal. The airport is located about 15 miles north of downtown Houston and is always open.

Lyndon B. Johnson Space Center
NASA Road exit off I-45 South
483-4321

The focal point of control for America's space flight pro-

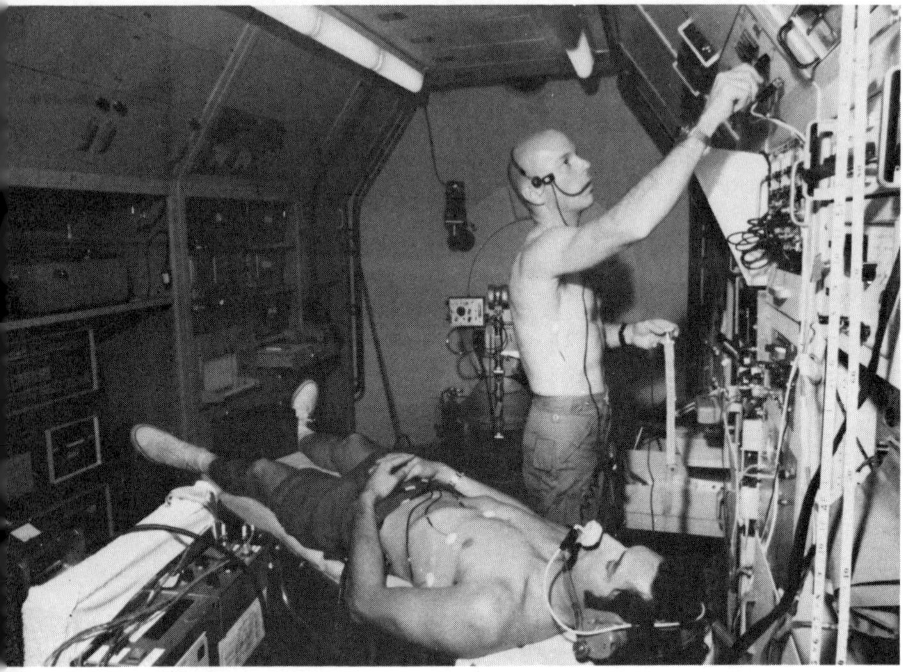

NASA scientists at Johnson Space Center conduct a cardio-pulmonary experiment for the Shuttle Spacelab program.

Part of a massive Saturn V rocket overwhelms smaller vehicles in NASA's Rocket Park.

Special Places : 79

The Lunar Module Test Article (LTA-8) was used in the Apollo program to train astronauts. Now it greets visitors to Building 2.

Mission Control at Johnson Space Center (Red Tour only).

gram is one of the most significant free attractions in Houston and the world. Two different self-guided tours begin at the Information Center, where you can see official NASA films and a truly awe-inspiring collection of exhibits including moon rocks, astronaut Gordon Cooper's Mercury space capsule, LEM (Lunar Exploration Module), Moon Rover, the Apollo 17 spacecraft, and many more too numerous to mention.

No reservations are needed to take the Green Tour, which is made available to the public every day of the year except Christmas. On this tour, you will see Mission Simulation and Training, where astronauts practice the complex maneuvers needed in the Skylab and Space Shuttle missions; Space Shuttle Orbiter Training, including full-scale Shuttle trainers; and the Lunar Sample Building, where hundreds of pounds of moon matter are being studied and analyzed by scientists. The greatest activity in most of these areas can be seen on weekdays before 4 P.M.

Reservations are required to take the Red Tour, which can be taken Monday through Friday except on federal holidays. To make a reservation, call 483-4321 or write to: NASA Johnson Space Center, Public Services Branch, AP4, Houston, TX 77058. The Red Tour includes visits to the Mission Control Center viewing room and the Space Environment Simulation Laboratory, where tests are made of space hardware in the world's largest vacuum chamber.

All tours are designed to accommodate the handicapped and everyone is invited to visit Rocket Park, where enormous multistage rockets can be studied up close. If you have any interest in space technology and exploration and are unfortunate enough to have but one day to spend sight-seeing in Houston, this is the place to go. There is nothing like it anywhere else in the world and it is well worth whatever time you have to spend. The Space Center is open from 9 A.M. to 4:30 P.M. every day of the year except Christmas.

Special Places : 81

An overview of Houston's Medical Center complex.

The Medical Center
North on Fannin or east on Holcombe from the intersection of Fannin and Holcombe
Drive or walk through one of the largest (and still growing) medical complexes in the world, currently consisting of 29 colleges, institutes, hospitals, and schools in addition to six more medical clinics and buildings. This was the site of the first successful artifical heart implant in the United States.

Maps and information are available at the parking booths when you enter. Entry is from Holcombe and Bertner drives, or off Fannin Street. Receive a parking slip from the gatekeeper and take a free 20-minute tour in your car. (Beyond 20 minutes, a fee will be assessed.)

NEWSPAPER TOURS

Houston Post
4747 Southwest Freeway
621-7000

Houston Chronicle
801 Texas Avenue
220-7171
See a big city newspaper go to press. Watch all the action involved in putting the paper to bed, from setting the type to rolling the presses to assembling the final copy. Both newspapers require reservations for their free tours. Since groups must be at least ten in number, call ahead to join a tour. Children under 12 are not included because of safety and supervision requirements.

Old Market Square
Travis, Milan, Congress, and Preston streets
Once the hub of Houston commerce, this area has undergone many changes over the years. Still significant for its architecture and history, it offers visitors a look at structures from two centuries in close proximity.

Old Sixth Ward—Sabine Historical District
Bounded by Houston and Washington avenues, Memorial Drive and Sawyer Street
This semiresidential and commercial area is on the northwest edge of downtown Houston. It contains a number of early Victorian gingerbread frame structures as well as **St. Joseph Catholic Church,** 1505 Kane Avenue, the first Catholic church north of the Buffalo Bayou. Here, Ernesto Martinez painted a large mural. The church is open for public viewing from 8 to 5 Monday through Friday.

Pennzoil Place
711 Louisiana
Two towers designed by Philip Johnson have made a

Visitors may watch the action in the Port of Houston's turning basin from the free observation platform at Wharf 9.

significant impact on the city skyline. Enter the glass-enclosed lobby and ride down to the Houston Underground shopping mall and tunnel.

Pioneer Memorial Log House
1510 Outer Belt (at Taub Loop)
This log structure is representative of pioneer homes built during the era of the Texas Republic. Maintained by the Daughters of the Republic of Texas, the cabin is open for public inspection on Sunday afternoon.

Port of Houston
Ship Channel I
672-8221
The Fabulous 50 Miles connect the Port of Houston to the Gulf of Mexico via the Ship Channel. More than $5 billion

has been invested in industrial facilities along the turning basin and Ship Channel. The turning basin at the eastern end of the channel can be seen from the observation platform at Wharf 9 (enter at Gate 8). An information-packed brochure entitled *The Port of Houston's Fabulous Fifty Miles* contains a detailed map of the entire port. It can be obtained by visiting or writing to: Port of Houston Executive Office, 1519 Capitol Avenue, P.O. Box 2562, Houston, TX 77001.

Visitors are welcomed aboard the vessel *Sam Houston*, which cruises around the turning basin and down the Ship Channel past some of the 4,000 ships that carry more than 55 million tons of cargo each year. For reservations and information about the free *Sam Houston* tours, call 225-0671.

Post Oak Central, I, II
2000 block of South Post Oak between San Felipe and Westheimer (off Loop 610 West)
This detailed Art Deco–style black and silver building was designed by Philip Johnson.

Sauer's Sausage Company
4406 Koehler
869-1438
The only packing house in Houston that uses no artificial preservatives in its products offers public tours of its facilities at 10 A.M. Monday through Friday. Interested visitors are asked to call one or two days in advance of the desired tour date. The company ships its products throughout the United States.

SHOPPING CENTERS

Because of Houston's suburban growth, its shopping centers are not only many in number but also large in size. In addition to the beautiful Galleria (discussed at greater

Shoppers at Sharpstown mall can spend a fortune or a pittance (or less) but still enjoy the comforts of a million-dollar spender.

length earlier in this chapter) there are many area centers of unique design with easy access to the shopper. The shopping malls are worthwhile places to visit not only for window shopping and relaxation but also for their singular personalities. The southwest area of the city has the greatest number of facilities—nearly half of the shopping centers and malls are located there.

Following is a list of the larger malls in Houston:

Almeda Mall, I-45 South, exit Almeda-Genoa Road. Enclosed mall with 72 stores and restaurants. Anchors are Foley's and J. C. Penney. (Southeast)

Baybrook Mall, I-45 South, exit Bay Area Boulevard. One hundred stores and restaurants. Anchors are Montgomery Ward, Joske's, and Sears. (Southeast)

The Galleria, 5015 Westheimer, west of South Post Oak and Loop 610 West. Multilevel enclosed shopping area features 252 businesses, including shops, restaurants, and two hotels, Galleria Plaza, and Houston Oaks. Major tenants are Lord & Taylor, Marshall Field, and Neiman Marcus. (Southwest)

Greenspoint Mall, I-45 North, exit Greens Road. Foley's, Sears, J.C. Penney, Montgomery Ward, and Lord & Taylor are among 134 shops.

Memorial City Mall, I-10 at Gessner exit. Enclosed mall with 67 shops and restaurants.

Northwest Mall, Loop 610 West, exit West 18th Street. Enclosed mall with 71 stores, restaurants, and major tenants Foley's and J.C. Penney. (Northwest)

Sharpstown Mall, Interstate 59 South, exit Bellaire. Enclosed mall's 136 stores include Foley's and Montgomery Ward. (Southwest)

Town & Country Village, on Memorial, exit West Belt from I-10 West. Joske's and Sakowitz are among the 120 stores and restaurants. (Southwest)

Westbury Mall, 5400 West Bellfort at Chimney Rock. Fifty-two specialty shops and restaurants. (Southwest)

Westwood Mall, U.S. 59 South, exit Bissonnet. Sixty-three stores and restaurants, including Joske's. (Southwest)

Following is a list of some of the larger shopping centers in Houston:

Allen Center, downtown location on Dallas and Smith streets, with 13 stores. (Downtown)

Bellaire Shopping District, on Bellaire Boulevard and Bissonnet, with 118 stores. (Southwest)

Carillion West, on Westheimer at Briar Park Drive west of Loop 610 West, with 100 stores. (Southwest)

Champions Village 3, FM 1960 at Mighty Oak Drive, with 30 stores. (Northwest)

Champions Village 1, FM 1960 at Champions Drive, with 24 stores. (Northwest)

Greenway Plaza—The Underground, 5 Greenway Plaza East, with 37 stores. (Southwest)

Humble Shopping District, Eastex Freeway and FM 1960, with 45 stores. (Humble)

Laura Koppe Shopping District, on Jensen at Laura Koppe, with 91 stores. (Northeast)

Northshore Village Shopping Center, on Northshore at Uvalde, with 64 stores. (Northeast)

Post Oak Center, on South Post Oak at Westheimer with 20 stores. (Southwest)

Post Oak Plaza, 1701 South Post Oak, with 15 stores. (Southwest)

River Oaks Shopping Center, West Gray at South Shepherd, with 56 stores. (Southwest)

Woodlake Square, on Westheimer at Gessner, with 22 stores. (Southwest)

Society for the Prevention of Cruelty to Animals
519 Studemont
869-8227
Small animals may be seen (and purchased at very nominal prices) at this facility of the SPCA. The shelter is open

88 : 500 THINGS TO DO IN HOUSTON FOR FREE

Following placement by the Voluntary Action Center of Houston and Harris County, a volunteer works one-to-one with a handicapped child to encourage and help her in developing language skills. Hundreds of volunteer opportunities are available.

Tuesday through Saturday from 9 to 5 and Sunday from 1 to 5. Closed on Monday.

Voluntary Action Center of Houston and Harris County
3100 Timmons Lane, Suite 100
965-0031
Here are more than 200 opportunities to do something for someone else—for free. The center has listings for various types of volunteer service at more than 200 nonprofit

social service agencies throughout the city. Although the Voluntary Action Center does not offer training to volunteer workers, most of the organizations it works with do. A weekly listing of nearly a dozen volunteer opportunities is published in the Sunday edition of the *Houston Post*. Call for additional details.

William F. Hobby Airport
Airport Road just west of I-45 South
Houston's first airport for commercial carriers is still in operation. It offers aviation fans a chance to view takeoffs and landings of modern aircraft along with the bustling ground preparations. Open daily.

CHAPTER 6

the libraries: city and county

Houston's libraries serve as repositories not only for literature but also for works of art, films, and audiovisual programs, and as sites for classes to enrich the mind and learn new skills. There are some 28 city libraries and about 18 county libraries. All have story hours and some craft activities for children. Summer reading programs are featured at all branch libraries.

Library cards are free for all Harris County residents. Applications may be obtained from the central library and all branches—city and county. Cards take about two weeks for processing, but a temporary card is available immediately. The key to all the free loan services the libraries have to offer, a card enables holders to borrow books, films, paintings, sculptures, records, and tapes.

The Central Library
Located at 500 McKinney, the Central Library's hours are 9 A.M. to 9 P.M. Monday through Friday, 9 A.M. to 6 P.M. Saturday, and 2 P.M. to 6 P.M. Sunday. The extensive film library is open from 10 A.M. to 6 P.M. Monday through Friday only. Information about all the library's holdings and events can be obtained by calling the public information office at 222-4456.

A number of regularly scheduled exhibits and pro-

In the connecting plaza between the new Central Public Library Building (pictured here) and the old edifice, is Claes Oldenburg's Geometric Mouse X.

grams are open to the public free of charge. A library card is not needed to attend these events (or to use materials within the library). The Lunch-Bunch meets on Wednesdays at noon for concerts, lectures, and demonstrations on a variety of topics in the Concourse Level Meeting Room. Tuesday Talkies are free films shown every Tuesday at 12:15 P.M., also in the Concourse Level Meeting Room. Story times for preschoolers are conducted on

Thursday morning at 10 and Saturday morning at 11. Grade school children between the ages of seven and 11 are invited to meet in the library at 11:30 A.M. on Saturdays. For adolescents between eight and 16, films are presented every Saturday at 2 P.M.

Three traveling Bookmobiles visit outlying areas not serviced by any branch libraries. For specific times and locations, call Bookmobile Service at 869-5161.

Branch Libraries
The newest library in the City of Houston system is the Collier, opening in mid-1981, displaying 47 years of memorabilia collected by Everett Collier, former editor of the *Houston Chronicle*. All the branches offer some free programs, exhibits, or classes. To keep abreast of the whirlwind schedule throughout the city system, pick up a Calendar of Events at the Main Library or any branch.

Northeast

Carnegie Branch
2211 Main
227-9177

Kashmere Gardens Branch
5411 Pardee
674-8461

Cliff Tuttle Branch
702 Kress at Lyons
675-4656

Lakewood Branch
8815 Feland
633-3725

Dixon Branch
8002 Hirsch
633-2147

Moody Branch
9525 Irvington
697-2745

Fifth Ward Branch
4014 Market Street
236-0759

Pleasantville Branch
1520 Gellhorn
676-0693

Northwest

Acres Homes Branch
8501 West Montgomery Road
448-9841

Heights Branch
1302 Heights Boulevard
861-4149

The Libraries: City and County : 93

Hillendahl Branch
2436 Gessner
467-9090

Kendall Branch
14330 Memorial
497-3590

Oak Forest Branch
1349 West 43rd
688-2251

Ring Branch
8835 Long Point Road
468-2643

Southeast

Bracewell Branch
10115 Kleckley
941-3130

Johnson Branch
3511 Reed Road
733-1983

Melcher Branch
7200 Keller
641-5611

Smith Branch
3624 Scott Street
741-6220

Stanaker Branch
611 69th Street
923-8784

Young Branch
6003 Beekman
643-8556

Park Place Branch
8145 Park Place Boulevard
645-4183

Southwest

Jungman Branch
5830 Westheimer
789-7211

Looscan Branch
2510 Willowick
622-6525

Meyer Branch
5005 West Bellfort
723-1630

Vinson Branch
3100 West Fuqua
433-0356

Walter Branch
7660 Clarewood & Fondren
771-5797

Harris County Libraries

Harris County Libraries offer most of the same services as the city of Houston libraries, from story hours for children to some craft classes. Check each library for particulars.

Harris County Libraries

Central Library
2301 Carolina
221-5350

Bookmobile
930 Corbindale
467-1590

Aldine Branch
11331 Airline
445-5560

Channelview Branch
531 Crockett
452-0181

Crosby Branch
5521 Avenue B
328-1313

Cypress Creek Branch
6815 Cypresswood Drive
376-3610

Fairbanks Branch
7122 North Gessner
466-4438

Freeman Memorial Branch
16602 Diana Lane
Clear Lake City
488-1906

Galena Park Branch
1702 3rd Street
674-2245

Highlands Branch
509 Stratford
Highland
426-4214

Humble Branch
111 West Higgins
Humble
446-3377

Jacinto City Branch
1026 Mercury
Jacinto City
673-3237

Katy Branch
5702 2nd Street
371-3509

LaPorte Branch
526 San Jacinto
LaPorte
471-4022

South Houston Branch
1013 Dallas
941-2385

Tomball Branch
701 James
Tomball
351-7269

Spring Memorial Branch
930 Corbindale
464-1633

West University Branch
6108 Auden
668-7180

Woodforest Branch
13601 Woodforest
453-8188

Clayton Library

Although it is not a part of the city or county system, the

Clayton Library Center for Genealogical Research, 5300 Caroline, provides a very special service entirely free of charge to more than 40,000 visitors each year. Here, a highly trained staff of librarians will help interested persons trace their family history using the largest collection of genealogical data in Texas, much of it on microfilm. For additional information and hours, call 524-0101.

CHAPTER 7

universities, galleries, and outdoor art

A cultural crazy quilt of campus sights and events, public sculptures, murals, fountains, and art galleries covers the greater Houston area. Partakers of this free, citywide, living museum will need to do plenty of traveling—much of it on foot—to enjoy all there is to see and do, but, with Houston's year-round semitropical climate, who can possibly complain?

THE UNIVERSITIES

Five major universities inside the Houston city limits are virtual cities within themselves. The campuses are dotted with contemporary and classical-style sculptures mingling with architecturally fascinating buildings on beautifully landscaped grounds. Each features a major library that is normally open to the public for research and leisure reading. (Generally, only students and faculty members are allowed to take out materials.)

More than just centers of academia, these universities sponsor concerts, recitals, and lecture series, some of which are free. They also house a number of major galleries and museums.

The Cullen Building is on the University of Houston Central Campus.

The University of Houston
3801 Cullen
The 330-acre Central Campus of the University of Houston system is located just off I-45 South (Gulf Freeway) at Cullen. A walking tour of the campus brings the visitor into contact with artworks and architecture that are blended into the landscape of this fine university, which became a four-year institution in 1934. Entering Gate 1 off Calhoun Boulevard, the visitor will find an information center where a free map and booklet describ-

ing the university can be obtained. From this point, the following sites and objects may be visited.

The Continuing Education Center—also houses the Conrad Hilton School of Restaurant and Hotel Management.

Wedgwood Collection—more than 50 original pieces—on the second floor of the Continuing Education Building. It was donated by George Kaphan.

Split-Level—a sculpture by Clement Mead Moore resting in front of the Continuing Education Building.

Ameristar—a sculpture by Jack Reyes commemorating America's Bicentennial.

Lynn Eusan Park—named for a student who was raped and murdered in the late 1960s.

Shasta's Cage—the home of a real live cougar, The University of Houston's mascot, Shasta.

The Galaxy Room of the Continuing Education Building is home for an eye-consuming sculptured wall hanging by Paul McClain celebrating the U.S. space program.

The Bruce Religion Center.

The Cullen Family Plaza.

Waterfall by L. Kelley—a fountain and sculpture. In the Cullen Family Plaza in front of Farrish Hall (College of Education).

Tower of Cheyenne by G. Knodel—located near the library.

Sandy in Defined Space by R. Miller—located near Agnes Arnold Hall.

A Model of the Moon and its Landscape made from actual sections of NASA photographs—located in the lobby of Science and Research.

The Fine Arts Complex.

Orpheus by G. Marcks—located at the entry gate to the Fine Arts Complex.

Hofheinz Pavilion—home of Cougar basketball and a unique in-ground bowl stadium.

University Center, the multitiered building where the following two artworks can be seen.

Abstract Figure by B. Fowler—located in the atrium of the University Center.

The Creation by David Hickman. An original mural in the style of Michelangelo portraying Walt Disney creating Mickey Mouse—University Center, third floor.

Although they are not a part of the self-guided tour, other noteworthy works of art on the University of Houston campus are as follows:

Big Orange by Willi Gutmann—General Service Building.

Big Sea by Brian Wall—College of Technology.

Bronze Head by Benin—East Office Annex.

Iroku by Sofu Teshighara—Agnes Arnold Hall.

Jonah & The Whale by Carroll Simms—Tennis Courts.

On 1969 by Menashe Kadishman—Entrance Number 6.

Orbit I by Masaru Takiguchi—Science and Research Building.

Orbit II by Masaru Takiguchi—Bates School of Law.

Round-A-Bout by Linda Howard—Department of Optometry.

Troika by Charles Ginnever—Science and Research Building.

Woman With Shawl by Francisco Zuniga—McElhinney Hall.

The M.D. Anderson Library is located in the tall building west of the University Center near Entrances 1 and 2 off Calhoun. Hours vary, depending on the number of courses in session at the university. Call 749-1883 or 749-1884 for details.

Once standing on prairie marshland, Rice University's Lovett Hall is just minutes from downtown Houston.

Rice University
6100 South Main Street
Looking much like an Ivy League school transplanted to the Southwest, the 300-acre campus is located about three miles south of downtown Houston. Founded in 1891 by William Marsh Rice (but not opened until 1912), the university has attained world acclaim for its emphasis on scientific study. After passing through the entrance gate sallyport on Main Street, the visitor is greeted by one architectural treat after another. Every building is unique and artful, with the overall architectural style blending Byzantine, Moorish, Spanish, and Italian forms.

A walking tour of the campus should include the following highlights: Allen Center, Lovett Hall, the statue of

William Marsh Rice, the Chemistry Building (the small front arcade is filled with sculptures), the Rice Media Center, the Rice Museum, Seawall Hall, Cohen House, Autry Court (home of Fighting Owl basketball), Rice Stadium (site of the 1973 NFL Super Bowl as well as Rice Owl football), and Rice Memorial Center and Chapel.

A free map of the campus can be obtained by calling 527-4929 or by visiting Room 326 in Allen Center Monday through Friday from 9 to 5. Enter the campus through Entrance 3 at Main and Outer Belt. The Fondren Library (527-4929) is located in the central portion of the campus. Hours are 7:40 A.M. to midnight Monday through Thursday, 7:40 A.M. to 10:00 P.M. Friday, 9 to 9 on Saturday, and 1 P.M. to midnight Sunday.

At various times during the year, free concerts of classical chamber music are performed at Hamman Hall at 8 P.M. A free schedule of musical offerings can be obtained at the Allen Center or by writing to: Shepherd School of Music, Rice University, Houston, TX 77001. Note that some concerts by world-renowned ensembles and guest artists have an admission fee. Concerts requiring a fee are clearly identified on the concert calendar.

Texas Southern University
3200 Cleburne
The youngest of Houston's major universities, Texas Southern was established in 1947 and has a present enrollment of 8,000. The library, located at 3201 Wheeler (phone: 527-7148), is noted for the Heartman Collection, the most comprehensive library of black history and culture in the Southwest. Hours are 8 A.M. to 11 P.M. Monday through Friday, 8:00 to 6:30 Saturday, and 2 to 8 Sunday. Also of note are the Barbara Jordan Archives and the African Cultural Art Collection.

Four notable works of art by Carroll H. Simms are displayed at various locations on the campus. They are: *African Queen Mother*, the Martin Luther King Center; *Jonah and the Whale*, New Education Building; *Man and*

Monkeys Reaching for the Moon is one of a number of contemporary sculptures by Carroll H. Simms on Texas Southern University's campus.

the Universe, Science Building; and Monkeys Reaching for the Moon, 2406 Wheeler Avenue. Before starting your tour, stop at the Campus Traffic and Security Office at 3017 Wheeler to obtain a free map of the campus and a visitor's parking permit.

Houston Baptist University
7502 Fondren Road
The 200-acre campus is composed of tightly grouped masonry buildings housing six colleges. The facilities include a fully equipped gymnasium, residence halls, an apartment complex, a 25,000-square-foot classroom building, and an academic quadrangle containing offices, classrooms, music rooms, a student center, a performance hall, a bookstore, and a cafeteria. The library is located at 7502 Fondren Road (phone: 774-7667). Hours for the library are 7:30 A.M. to 10:00 P.M. Monday through Friday, 1 to 5 Saturday, and 2 to 10 Sunday.

The speakers' program, originated and funded by students, has been open to the public since its origination in 1971. The series brings a nationally known speaker to campus each week. In addition to delivering a formal assembly speech, the guest meets with students over coffee in the cafeteria or at a noon luncheon and often visits classrooms. Other traditional events—the bonfire, tug-of-war, Westward Ho Days, snowball fight, and Homecoming—are also planned and entirely operated by the students. Further information about the speakers' series and other events can be obtained by calling 774-7661, ext. 209–210.

University of St. Thomas
3812 Montrose
Founded in 1947 by the Roman Catholic Church, this four-year university has been endowed with gifts that have enhanced its architectural beauty. Five sculptures by Tony Smith are located on Mulberry Street at Branard: *New Piece, Marriage, The Snake Is Out, Elevens Are Up,*

and *Spitball*. In addition to these notable sculptures are two canvases by Joe Overstreet: *Ancestral God* and *Free Direction*. Both are located in Cullen Hall (the music building). The Doherty Library is open from 8 A.M. to midnight Monday through Thursday, 8 A.M. to 6 P.M. Friday, 9 to 4 Saturday, and 1 P.M. to midnight Sunday. Phone: 522-7912. The small St. Thomas campus is located near downtown Houston, and its continuity with city streets forms part of its beauty.

ART GALLERIES

All but a few of the galleries listed in this section are privately owned, profit-oriented businesses where the artworks on display are for sale. Most galleries are tolerant of well-mannered browsers. Those listed here are a representative sample of the many galleries in the Houston area.

>**Art League of Houston,** 1953 Montrose, 523-9530; 10 to 4 Monday through Friday, 12 to 4 Saturday. Included in the program is a variety of media exhibits, all juried. The largest showing is called "Dimension Houston," always held in December.
>
>**Cronin Gallery,** 2008 Peden, 526-2548; 10 to 6 Tuesday through Saturday. The gallery is devoted exclusively to fine photography.
>
>**The Crows Nest Art Gallery,** 230 Jefferson (in LaPorte), 471-4371; 10 to 6 Tuesday through Saturday by appointment. Works by area artists are displayed in unusual surroundings. Indian jewelry is also shown.
>
>**Deep River Armory,** 5700 Star, 667-4440; 10 to 5 Monday through Friday. A large collection of military memorabilia and artifacts such as insignias, buttons, and uniform components is displayed.
>
>**Du Bose Gallery,** 2950 Kirby, 526-4916; 9 to 5:30 Monday through Friday, 11 to 4:30 Saturday. In addition to representing a number of well-known regional talents, the gallery also has major exhibits of works by international artists.

Universities, Galleries, and Outdoor Art : 105

Editions, Inc., 1800 South Post Oak Road, 871-9290; 10 to 5 Monday through Saturday. Limited-edition prints are the house specialty.

Galveston Arts Center on the Strand, 2116½ Strand, Galveston, 763-0613; 8 to 5 Monday through Friday, 11 to 4 Saturday, and 1 to 4 Sunday. It's located in the old First National Bank of Galveston building in the heart of the historic district.

Gerhard Wurzer Gallery, Galleria II, 961-9888; 10 to 9 Monday through Friday, 10 to 6 Saturday. The gallery features prints of works by the Old Masters, especially from 19th-century France.

Hanson Galleries, 9039 Westheimer, 977-1242; 10 to 6 Monday through Saturday (open until 9 P.M. on Thursdays only). It specializes in unusual art objects, including fine woodcrafts.

M. E.'s Gallery, 1408 Michigan (off Waugh), 527-8862; 10 to 4 or by appointment Tuesday through Saturday. The gallery displays a wide variety of fine crafts from pottery to jewelry created by local, state, and national artists.

Meredith Long Gallery, 2323 San Felipe, 523-6671; 10 to 6 Tuesday through Saturday. The specialty is 19th-century American art, concentrating on sports themes, but other works are also displayed.

Millioud Gallery, 4041 Richmond, 621-3330; 10 to 4 Monday through Friday, 10 to 5 Saturday. An interesting gallery for young collectors, it features contemporary prints, drawings, and watercolors.

Moody Gallery, 2015-J West Gray, 526-9911; 10 to 5:30 Tuesday through Saturday. Artists from Texas and the Houston area in particular are well represented.

Robinson Galleries, 1200 Bissonnet, 521-9221; 10:00 to 5:30 Tuesday through Saturday. The emphasis is on 19th- and 20th-century American art. Regional contemporary work in a variety of media is also shown.

Texas Southern University's Gallery of Traditional African Art, 3201 Wheeler (in the library), 527-7121 or 527-7326; 8 A.M. to 11 P.M. Monday through Friday. Guided tours can be arranged by appointment.

Toni Jones Gallery, 1200 Bissonnet, 528-7998; 9 to 6 or by appointment Monday through Saturday. The gallery presents artworks and photographs by emerging and established artists.

Watson-DeNagy Gallery, 1106 Berthea, 526-9883; 11 to 5 Tuesday through Saturday. Displays of contemporary American art are changed monthly.

OUTDOOR ARTWORKS

As a city grows, statues and fountains begin to spring up as part of the landscape. Some are memorials, while others are clearly works of art. As you travel in the Houston area, the works described below will suddenly appear, often when you least expect them; a corner of a city block or an esplanade becomes an oasis for fine art. A number of the most renowned sculptors of yesterday and today—including Henry Moore, Auguste Rodin, Gutzon Borgland, Alexander Calder, and many others—have major works displayed in Houston, where they are always ready to brighten the travels of residents and visitors alike.

Sam Houston
Astride his horse atop a marble archway, General Houston points the way downtown along the longest main street in the world. The most famous statue in Houston is in Hermann Park at Fannin and Hermann drives.

Mecom Memorial Fountain
Located just south of the Warwick Hotel, 5701 Main Street, this beautiful three-section fountain actually serves as a major component in the cooling system of the famed hotel.

Peggy
At Main and Richmond, a petite bronze statue of a young girl near a cascading waterfall was created by Gutzon Borgland, the scupltor of the Mount Rushmore Memorial.

A well-known landmark of the city named in his honor is the statue of Sam Houston in Hermann Park.

Spindle Piece, a sculpture by Henry Moore, is on the north side of Allen Parkway just west of downtown Houston.

Abesti Gorgora V
This 50-ton sculpture was placed on the Museum of Fine Arts lawn in 1966 and has been viewed in awe by thousands of visitors annually ever since. The same area is the site for no less than ten other major artworks:

Around, by Alexander Liberman

The Crab, by Alexander Calder

Hercules Upholding the Heavens, by Paul Manship

Pieta, by Charles Umlauf

Sculpture on Garden Bench, by Willaim McVey

Space, Concept, Nature, by Lucio Fontana

Stairway to "V," by Ben Woitena

Untitled, by Clark Murray

The Walking Man, by Auguste Rodin

Colloquio Col Vento, by Pietro Consagra

William Marsh Rice
A statue of William Marsh Rice, the founder of Rice University, whose ashes are entombed at the base, is located at 600 South Main Street.

America Mural
When you're in the downtown area, walk into the second level of the Bank of the Southwest Building, 910 Travis, and look at this 45-by-15-foot mural depicting America's heritage.

The Family
Located near the Old Prudential Building at Holcombe and Fannin, this sculpture and fountain is a powerful reminder of the richness of family life and a symbol for the National Parents and Teachers Association.

The Healer
An enormous mosaic on the front facade of Methodist Hospital, 6565 Fannin, depicts Jesus working with practitioners of the medical profession.

St. Luke's Hospital Award for Excellence
At the Bates Street entrance to St. Lukes Hospital, off Bertner Street, this rose granite and marble heart is a graceful symbol of the dedicated efforts of cardiovascular specialists and their teams, who made medical history right here in Houston.

Miscellaneous Pieces

Atropos Key, by Hannah Stewart—Miller Theatre, Hermann Park

Axis, by Frank Maguire—Multi-Service Center, 1778 Heights Boulevard

Dancer, by Marcello Mascherini—Jones Hall, 615 Louisiana

Gemini II, by Richard Lippold—Jones Hall, 615 Louisiana

Pair of Horses, by Bob Fowler—Jones Hall, 615 Louisiana

Figure of Christ, Tannie Pizzitola Memorial—Sacred Heart Co-cathedral, 1111 Pierce

Figure of Christ, Carter Raia Memorial—Sacred Heart Co-cathedral, 1111 Pierce

Other Public Fountains

Charlotte Allen Fountain, Baldwin Park, Elgin at Crawford

Bird Fountain, Hermann Park

Brownie Fountain, Hermann Park Zoo

Fragrant Garden Fountain, Hermann Park

Geyser Fountain, Cullen Center Green, Smith at Calhoun

Houston Lighting & Power Fountains, Energy Control Center Plaza, Walker at Louisiana

Hyde Park Fountain, Hyde Park at Waugh

Libertard, by Hannah Stewart, World Trade Center, 1520 Texas Avenue

Little Mecom Fountain, one block north of Warwick Hotel on Main Street

Mecom-Rockwell Fountain, Hermann Park

Rain Forest Waterfall, Hermann Park Zoo

River Oaks Fountain, River Oaks Park, 3600 Locke Lane

Scanlan Fountain, Sam Houston Park

Lillian Schnitzer Memorial Fountain, Rose Garden in Hermann Park

Bob Smith Memorial Fountain, Smith and Leland

Westbury Square Fountain, Westbury Square Shopping Center, Bellfort near Post Oak

Whitehall Fountain, Whitehall Hotel Plaza, 1700 Smith

Gus Wortham Fountain, Allen Parkway

CHAPTER 8

music, films, and plays

Houston's cultural scene is greatly enhanced by the overwhelming variety of free shows staged at the famous Miller Outdoor Theatre. The theatre offers something for everyone's musical taste from spring until fall. The wide-ranging program provides considerable solace to anyone dispairing over the fact that only a handful of other free concerts are performed with any degree of regularity anywhere else in the city. Seasonal events are discussed in chapter 9.

Miller Outdoor Theatre
Outer Belt and Hermann Circle Drive (in Hermann Park)
Recorded information: 222-3576
Miller Theatre is the largest city-owned institution of its kind in the nation to offer free programs of first-rate performing arts. Located on 7½ tree-shaded acres in Hermann Park, it is visited by more than 260,000 people each year. Spectators crowd into the seats within the pavilion or spread their blankets on the grassy hill extending far beyond the stage.

Almost every type of performance imaginable takes place under the stars on a number of evenings each week, usually starting at 8:30 P.M. The famed Houston

Music, Films, and Plays : 113

Concert fans at the Miller Theatre enjoy picnic dinners and the Houston Symphony . . .

. . . or arrive early for seating inside the pavilion.

Symphony plays a variety of orchestral works. The Theatre Under the Stars performs Broadway musicals on a grand scale. Space/Dance/Theatre puts on contemporary rock ballets directed by James Clouser. SUM concerts feature blues and jazz at one end of the musical spectrum while performances by the Houston Ballet and the Houston Grand Opera offer a different type of musical spectacle.

During August, the University of Houston and the city sponsor the annual Houston Shakespearean Festival, when full performances of some of the Bard's greatest works are staged. A free film festival is usually held in October. (In 1980 more than 30 free films were screened, including *Gone with the Wind* and other favorites directed by Hitchcock, featuring the Marx Brothers, and Bogart, as well as more contemporary productions such as *Breaking Away* and *Dr. Strangelove.*) The Houston Folk Festival is generally held in September, the Opera Festival sometime in spring, and the June Teenth Blues Festival during the week of June 19. Times for the Jazz Festival seem to be as jumpy as the music, but September looks like the best bet. Recorded announcements describing the current fare can be heard by calling 222-3576.

Seating is generally on a first-come basis, but tickets are required for pavilion seating during opera, ballet, Shakespeare, and Theatre Under the Stars performances. Free tickets are available at the theatre box office, which is open from 11:30 to 1:00 on the day of a performance.

University of Houston
Central Campus Instrumental Ensembles
More than 100 student and faculty recitals and in excess of 20 major concerts are offered without charge each year by the University of Houston School of Music. For information on specific events and times, call the School of Music at 749-3796.

Houston Municipal Band
Various locations throughout Houston
From April through August, free concerts in local parks and playgrounds are sponsored by the City Parks and Recreation Department and the Cultural Arts Council of Houston. The performances are made possible by a grant from the Music Performance Trust Fund in cooperation with the American Federation of Musicians Local 65. For specific program information, call 222-3485 or 222-5525.

Houston Civic Symphony
Houston Baptist University
This surprisingly good musical group is composed entirely of adult volunteers. Rehearsals at Houston Baptist University are open to the public every Tuesday evening from September through May at 7:30. During the same period, free public concerts are given at various locations throughout the city. For more information, call 682-6767.

Houston Symphony
Jones Hall, 615 Louisiana
224-4240; ask for Ginny Cade
In addition to free concerts at Miller Theatre during the summer, the famed Houston Symphony offers eight very special days of musical entertainment during the winter. The Open Rehearsals offer the only free opportunity to see the orchestra in its winter headquarters.

Picnic with a Star is held on four Mondays during the September-through-May winter concert season. The concerts run from approximately noon to 1 in the Jones Hall lobby, and visitors are invited to bring a picnic lunch and meet the world-famous guest artists. Call for specific dates.

Open Rehearsals on four Fridays from noon to 1, also during the winter season, give concert fans an opportunity to hear the inner workings of the orchestra. Again, you will need to call the orchestra office for specific dates.

CHAPTER 9

annual dos

The emphasis is on fun for the entire family at dozens of regularly scheduled annual events held throughout the Houston area. To keep abreast of those one-of-a-kind and sporadic happenings that are planned from time to time, try consulting the Thursday editions of the Houston *Chronicle* and *Post*. *Houston City* magazine, a monthly publication available at most newsstands for $1.75, includes information on seasonal and changing events. When you hear an enticing tidbit about some event but can't quite catch the details on where and when, you might be able to find additional information at the Houston Convention and Visitors Council, 1522 Main (658-4200), as well as at the Houston Chamber of Commerce, 1100 Milam (651-1313).

JANUARY
Memorial City Shopping Center Art Show
During mid-month, artists from throughout the United States exhibit their works in the mall. Off I-10 West at Gessner exit; 464-8640.

Almeda and Northwest Malls
The annual winter antique show, Something Old, Some-

thing New, Something Special, Something Blue, is held in mid-January; also, "Luv ya Blue" Oilers salute.

FEBRUARY
Houston Federation of Garden Clubs Show
Always beautiful floral displays are exhibited in the Hermann Park Garden Center at 1500 Hermann Drive; 529-5371.

Houston Livestock and Rodeo Parade
At 9:15 on the opening day of the Houston Rodeo, covered wagons, marching bands, and more than 6,000 horses convene at Rusk and Main. Many have come to town after extensive trail rides. As always, there will be huge crowds, lots of local color, and "Go Texas" enthusiasm from every quarter.

Almeda and Northwest Malls
Fiddler's Festival, western fashions, a pickup truck–stuffing contest, music, and art are all part of the fun at the Lone Star Celebration.

MARCH
St. Patrick's Day Parade
Many of Houston's real and honorary descendants of Ireland put on a bit of the Green and march from Rusk to Main to Polk to Travis to Walker to Begley in the downtown district, stepping off at 9:30 A.M. For a permit to enter the parade, contact the Ancient Order of Hibernians, 1740 W. 27th Street, Suite 309, Houston, TX 77008; or call 868-3680. You'll be green with envy if you miss the memorial service, Irish dancing, bagpipe music, speeches, and fun that are scheduled each year after the parade at the statue of Dick Dowling in Herman Park.

Houston Festival
A celebration of the city focusing on the arts spans the last two weekends of the month. The festival features outdoor

Alabama-Coushatta Indians perform in Sam Houston Park during the Houston Festival.

performances on eight stages, including free concerts as well as dances by the Alabama-Coushatta Indians, monumental visual arts projects, juried craft shows, and a street bash around Old Market Square. The festivities unfold in various downtown public and private spaces, from Sam Houston Park to City Hall to Jones Plaza to Old Market Square. Additional details can be obtained from the Houston Festival Office by calling 521-9329.

Custom Car Show
See the latest in automotive funk and flash at this exhibit, which is normally held during the last weekend in March

at the Memorial City Shopping Center, off I-10 West at Gessner exit; 464-8640.

Bellaire Ethnic Folk Festival
Houston's city within a city (Bellaire is almost in the heart of Houston) sponsors this event at the esplanade park at Rice and Bellaire boulevards. For specific times and additional information, call the Bellaire Chamber of Commerce at 666-1521.

Almeda and Northwest Malls
Bagpipers, a spring fashion show, and a contest for a free trip to Ireland are part of the "Pack Your Bags" theme for mid-March.

APRIL
Houston Amaryllis Show
The spectacular floral exhibit is sponsored by the Houston Amaryllis Society at the Hermann Park Garden Center, 1500 Hermann Drive. For specific times, call 529-5371.

Small Games Tournament
Spectators can always watch these contests sponsored by the Houston Parks and Recreation Department, without charge, but there is a fee to enter the tournament. For times, locations, and additional details, call 222-3401, 520-7004, or 641-4111.

University of Houston Free Fair
The university sponsors nearly nine hours of free rock music, normally on the last Friday of the month, at the Free Fair held at Lynn Euson Park on the central campus. Food is for sale and hours are from noon to 9. Phone: 749-1435.

San Jacinto Day
April 21 is the anniversary of Texas' independence from

Mexico. At the San Jacinto Battleground, a full-dress pageant reenacts some of the events from the year 1836.

Bellaire Relics and Antiques Festival
Half of Bellaire seems to display their treasures and junk at Rice and Bellaire boulevards. For specific dates and times, call 666-1521.

Almeda and Northwest Malls
An Easter theme is developed in the Fiesta of Flowers, which extends from the beginning to the middle of the month.

MAY
Bonsai Society Show
The Oriental art of tree shaping forms the basis of a fascinating show at the Hermann Park Garden Center, 1500 Hermann Drive; 529-5371.

The Houston Garden Center in Hermann Park is home for the Bonsai Society Show in May.

SPCA Mutt Show

Dogs entered into any of a large number of often comic categories are judged by jurists who scoff at pedigrees. Held on the final day of Be Kind to Animals Week, usually the first week in May, the show has easy entry requirements that do not involve an entry fee. The society is at 517 Studemont; 869-8227.

Police Week

You will need to check newspapers for specific details, but the action usually begins late in May at the downtown station, 61 Reasoner Street. Included in the displays are the latest crime-fighting gadgets, helicopters, motorcycles, and SWAT team demonstrations; even the canine corps gets into the act.

Industrial Arts Fair

On the Thursday, Friday, and Saturday before Mother's Day, exhibits prepared by students from the Spring Branch High Schools are shown and judged at the Memorial City Shopping Center. Off I-10 West at Gessner exit; 464-8640.

Cinco de Mayo

The Fifth of May celebration observed by the Mexican-American community honors the Battle of Pueblo, in which French invaders were defeated by the Mexican army in 1862. Watch local newspapers for specific events.

Almeda and Northwest Malls

A school open house and fashion show are part of May Daze, a pre–Mother's Day salute to moms. A summer art show is the highlight of "Color it May," held during the last week of the month.

JUNE

Annual MG Car Show

The little cars are exhibited on the Thursday, Friday, and

Saturday before Father's Day at Memorial City Shopping Center. Off I-10 West at the Gessner exit; 464-8640.

June Teenth Blues Festival
Blues music is played at the Miller Theatre during the week of June 19th.

JULY

Fourth of July Celebrations
Major displays are held on July 3 or 4 in Hermann Park, the Sharpstown Shopping Center, the Belle Park Shopping Center in Alief, near the Stafford City Hall in Stafford, and Greenspoint Mall.

At Bagby and Allen Parkway in Sam Houston Park, a Fourth of July celebration from 1 to 5 features bands, antique cars, and VFW festivities. The Bellaire July 4 Parade can be seen, among other places, from the esplanade park at Rice and Bellaire boulevards. For specific times and parade routes, call the Bellaire Chamber of Commerce at 666-1521 prior to the holiday.

Almeda and Northwest Malls
The Mickey Mouse Festival in early July features Mickey, Minnie, Goofy, and Pluto in three shows daily for the entire ten-day run.

AUGUST

Houston Shakespearean Festival
The play's the thing during a whole series of free evening performances at the Miller Theatre.

Bromeliad Show and Sale
Bromeliaceous plants belong to the pineapple family, and many species sport stiff leaves, spikes, and colorful flowers. Held during the third weekend in August at the Houston Arboretum and Botanical Garden, 4501 Wood-

way, from 10 A.M. to 5 P.M. Free lectures on plant care are given at 10, 2, and 4; 681-8433.

Blessing of the Shrimp Fleet
The festivities begin at 2 P.M. on the first weekend in August at the Kemah-Galveston Bay Channel near the Kemah Bridge; 474-4792.

Lapidary Society and Houston Aquarium Society
Each organization runs a week-long display at Memorial City Shopping Center. Off I-10 West at Gessner exit; 464-8640.

Almeda and Northwest Malls
Class Action held during the first two weeks of August features junior fashion shows, Safety City, and Storybook Theater for children.

SEPTEMBER

University of Houston Free Fair
The April music and food extravaganza makes an encore appearance for fall. See the April listing for details.

Fiestas Patrias
Celebrating Mexico's independence from Spain, a colorful downtown parade and other events at various locations are sponsored by Houston's Mexican-American community. Watch local papers for details.

Houston Folk Festival
Folk music fills the evening air at the Miller Outdoor Theatre.

Almeda and Northwest Malls
The much requested Antique Show and Sale makes a fall reappearance during mid-September.

OCTOBER

University of Houston Beauty Bowl
An all-women's football game is held at Robertson Stadium on the University of Houston Central Campus, usually on Thursday evening during the third week of the month (just before University of Houston homecoming). Depending on your point of view, plenty of humorous and/or sexist comments are made by the stadium announcer. For details, call 749-1435.

Free Film Festival
Dozens of classic and fairly modern motion pictures are shown at the Miller Outdoor Theatre. Detailed schedules are available at the theatre box office. For information, call 222-3576.

Woodcarvers Show
Fascinating exhibits of woodcraft can be seen at the Memorial City Shopping Center. Off I-10 West at Gessner exit; 464-8640.

Greek Festival
Enjoy a free tour of the Annunciation Greek Orthodox Cathedral at 3511 Yoakum. Admission is charged for other festivities.

Westbury Square Sidewalk Art Show
Centered around 542 Westbury Square (off Bellfort Street and Chimney Rock), this show features the work of local artists.

Almeda and Northwest Malls
Arts and crafts and diverse entertainment are part of The Great American Hometown Fair held during the middle weekend of the month. Trick-or-treaters are welcomed at all mall stores during the Halloween Haunt held on the 31st.

NOVEMBER

Foley's Thanksgiving Day Parade
A gala event sponsored for three decades by Foley's Department Store, the parade begins at 10 A.M. on Thanksgiving Day, moving down Main Street from Rusk and back onto Travis.

Rose Show
On one day only, when the lovely flowers are at their finest, the Memorial City Shopping Center features a magnificent display of roses that will be remembered long after the blush is gone. Call 464-8640 for specific times. A major art exhibit, featuring works by Texas and American artists, is also held at the shopping center during November.

Almeda and Northwest Malls
Christmas in a Nutshell, held from November 21 through December 31, features seasonal decor and special window displays throughout the mall based on *The Nutcracker Suite*.

DECEMBER

The Messiah
Performed by the Houston Youth Symphony and sponsored by the Baptist Churches of Greater Houston, George Frederick Handel's famed oratorio can be enjoyed during the weekend before Christmas at Jesse H. Jones Hall. For specific times, call 222-3561.

Candlelight Tours of Sam Houston Park
Free guided tours of the park and historic homes are conducted Tuesday through Saturday evenings at 7 for several weeks just before Christmas. (For a discussion of the historic buildings, see the Houston Heritage Society, chapter 3.) On Christmas Eve, carols are sung at the bandstand.

CHAPTER 10

historic Galveston

Galveston is the Miami Beach of Texas, an island city with more than 30 miles of sandy beaches along the warm waters of the Gulf of Mexico. Its history is as colorful as its palm-and-oleander-lined boulevards. The first European settlement on the island was established by the pirate Jean Laffite in 1817, and Galveston soon developed into a thriving commercial and resort community. Magnificent mansions were erected as the first telegraph and electric lights in Texas came to the island.

In 1900 floodwaters brought by a disastrous hurricane completely inundated the island. Thomas Edison rushed by train to take early motion pictures of the devastation in which more than 5,000 people were killed. As Galveston's residents dug out of the debris, work was started on a massive seawall that today extends for ten miles along the island's southern beaches. Extensive reconstruction efforts were undertaken to refurbish the expensive buildings damaged by the floodwaters. In the last several decades, the seawall has withstood numerous challenges from raging hurricanes, but homes built on stilts or with high first floors on the Texas mainland just across Galveston Bay testify to the fact that this is hurricane country.

Nearly two million out-of-state visitors flock to Galveston each year, making the island the most popular resort area on the Gulf of Mexico.

Within an hour's drive of downtown Houston via the Gulf Freeway, Galveston is now a highly commercialized resort area catering to visitors from throughout southeast Texas and beyond. Fine hotels, restaurants, sight-seeing extravaganzas, and amusement centers afford the visitor plenty of ways to spend money. Probably the most famous of all the Christmas festivals in Texas, Dickens' Evening on the Strand until a few years ago was free to all visitors to Galveston. Now an admission fee of several dollars is charged.

Despite the commercialism, the island offers several dozen fascinating places to see and things to do that can be enjoyed without charge. If you plan extensive sight-seeing on Galveston Island, you will undoubtedly want to spend the few dollars required to see such attractions as Sea-Arama or Seawolf Park or to tour the interiors of a number of grand old mansions.

To the visitor unfamiliar with the many delights of Galveston, the first stop should be the Visitor Information Center at Seawall Boulevard and 21st Street. Here you can obtain free maps of the island and brochures covering just about everything the resort has to offer. To reach the center from downtown Houston, take the Gulf Freeway (I-45/75) south across Galveston Bay to the 61st Street exit (West Beach). Turn right and drive south until you reach Seawall Boulevard. Turn left (east) on Seawall and drive to 21st Street. The Visitor Information Center will be on your left, in the ground floor of the Moody Civic Center. During the summer, the center is generally open from 8:30 to 7:00 on weekdays, but weekend and winter hours can vary. Find out about specific hours by calling 763-4311.

PLACES TO VISIT IN GALVESTON

American National Insurance Company Tower
One Moody Plaza
763-4661
Galveston's only skyscraper is the headquarters of the largest insurance company in Texas. The Archives on the 20th floor is surrounded on all four sides by clear glass walls enabling visitors to see for 30 miles in every direction. All of Galveston Island can easily be seen from this vantage point, which is even more enjoyable if you bring binoculars. A sizable collection of historic photographs, etchings, and paintings is also on display on the 20th floor. Some of the large murals show the destruction of the island in the 1900 hurricane, the building of the seawall, and many of the historic mansions scattered around the island. The observation room is open free to the public from 2 to 4 seven days a week from June through

August and on weekdays only from September through May.

The American National Insurance Co. also boasts that it has one of the largest corporate collections of fine art in the world scattered throughout its 20-story building. Artists represented include Audubon, Beale, Calder, Rockwell, Warhol, Whistler, and many others. Free tours of the collection are given Monday through Friday. For further information, call 763-4661, ext. 216.

Bolivar Ferry
Highway 87 at Galveston Channel
The Texas Department of Highways and Public Transportation operates large diesel ferries that carry pedestrians and autos from Galveston to Point Bolivar. The ferries leave every 20 minutes around the clock and have observation decks, rest rooms, and car ports and offer a great place to take in all of Galveston Harbor. Children enjoy feeding the sea gulls that often sail with the ships. If you have taken your car on the free excursion, you can drive to the old lighthouse at Bolivar, about a mile beyond the landing. Built in 1872 and one of the few such structures to survive the hurricanes pounding the Texas coast over the years, the lighthouse was once used to guide great clipper ships into Galveston Harbor.

East End Historic District
Around 15th and Winnie
This entire area of more than 30 square blocks contains at least 100 notable homes, many of which have been painstakingly restored to revive their former elegance. Some of the Greek Revival–style homes were built as long ago as the 1850s, and the entire district has become a National Historic Landmark. To enjoy a self-guided walking tour to the fullest, be sure to pick up a free brochure entitled *East End Historic District Association* at the

130 : 500 THINGS TO DO IN HOUSTON FOR FREE

Bike routes through the East End Historic District are clearly marked with directional signs. The area contains at least 100 fine Victorian homes.

Galveston Visitor Information Center. The brochure includes a map and sometimes detailed listings of an even 100 homes in the district.

Galveston Beaches
Automotive congestion was once a serious problem in some stretches of Galveston's 32 miles of sandy beaches,

Popular Stewart Beach is on the eastern end of Galveston Island.

but new traffic and parking controls have greatly improved the situation. (When surf is up, it is still almost impossible to avoid horrendous traffic jams, however, as Houstonites flock to the beaches with surfboards in tow.) Free parking can generally be found just about everywhere along Seawall Boulevard, but fees are charged at some lots.

The most popular beach on Galveston is Stewart Beach, which is near Broadway (south of Seawall Boulevard) and East Beach. Lifeguards are always on duty during the 9 A.M. to 9 P.M. summer hours.

Galveston County Historical Museum
2219 Market Street
766-2340
Exhibits relating the history of the Galveston area, including the Karankawa Indians, Jean Laffite, the Battle of Galveston in the Civil War, the rise and fall of the Strand financial district, and more are housed in the former City National Bank Building, which is noted for its painted ceilings and brass chandeliers. Hours are 8:30 to 4:00 on weekdays, 9:30 to 4:30 on Saturdays, and 1 to 5 on Sundays.

Mosquito Fleet
Near Moody Street at the Galveston Channel
Galveston's Fisherman's Wharf is the home for a virtual armada of small shrimp trawlers that generally bring in more than 100,000 pounds of shrimp daily. Large fish markets along the wharf sell fresh flounder, oysters, crabs, and, of course, shrimp. You can watch all the action from Pier 19. The entire north shore of the island from 9th Street to 41st Street encompasses the Port of Galveston. Here, interested sight-seers can watch ships from around the world docking at America's most accessible harbor.

Rosenberg Library
2310 Sealy Avenue
763-8854
The oldest free public library in Texas houses artifacts from many prominent historic figures, including Jean Lafitte, Sam Houston, and Stephen Austin. The library also features an art collection and rare books. Hours are 9 to 9 Monday through Thursday, 9 to 6 Friday and Saturday. Closed Sundays.

The Seawall
Along the Gulf of Mexico
As you drive east on Seawall Boulevard from 61st Street, Galveston's famous Seawall will be to your immediate right. Extensive beach areas, fishing piers, restaurants, and hotels follow the line of the wall, which, at low tide, rises 17 feet or more above the level of the Gulf of Mexico. At various locations along the north side of Seawall Boulevard you may notice high earthen mounds with concrete facades facing the gulf. Now covered with grass and wildflowers, these structures were actually artillery and observation pillboxes built by the United States in World War I (and used again during World War II) to monitor shipping activities in the gulf and to protect against naval invasion.

Separating the beaches from the inland portions of the island, the Seawall provides one of the world's longest sidewalks and is a popular place for strolling, bicycling, skateboarding, and roller skating. Bicycles and roller skates can be rented at many establishments along the boulevard.

The Strand
Around Strand and 22nd Street
During the latter half of the 19th century, the area along the Strand and Mechanic Street between 20th and 25th streets was the most important economic center in Texas.

Like many other structures in the Strand district, the Rice, Baulard & Company Building, built in 1870, has been completely restored.

Once known as "the Wall Street of the Southwest," the Strand, lined with iron-front buildings painted to resemble masonry, started to decline with the advent of the 20th century.

Today the often elaborate buildings lining both sides of the street have been restored carefully, and the entire district has been designated a National Historic Landmark. Art galleries, gift shops, ice cream parlors, government and private offices, and other commercial establishments operate within the Victorian buildings, whose famous iron facades are illuminated in the evening by gaslights on both sides of the street.

The Strand Visitors Center, at 2014 Strand, will provide tourists with a number of free brochures describing the historic district. The center also presents free screenings of the motion picture *Galveston: The Golden Age of the Gilded Isle*, as well as an audiovisual presentation about the *Elissa*, a square-rigged ship built in 1877 and currently undergoing restoration at Pier 22.

Free walking tours of the Strand district are given by the Galveston Historic Foundation on Saturday at noon and Sunday at 2. The foundation is headquartered in the second floor of the same historic building housing the Strand Visitors Center.

Texas Heroes Monument
Broadway at 25th Street
The story of Texas's war with Mexico is highlighted on bronze plaques around the base of the statue, which was completed in 1900.

OUTDOOR ACTIVITIES IN GALVESTON

Swimming, fishing, and beachcombing are probably the most popular outdoor pursuits on Galveston, but bicycling, roller skating, skateboarding, bird-watching, and camping can also be enjoyed without charge. People

The Galveston Arts Center is visible at far left in this group of three restored buildings along 22nd St. between Strand and Mechanic.

lucky enough to own seaworthy ships or boats capable of sailing the waters of the gulf can launch them at free boat ramps located at 35th, 59th, and 61st streets. A number of municipal parks on the island provide free facilities for tennis, softball, shuffleboard, and basketball. Roller skating and skateboarding are permitted all along the Seawall, but real aficionados tend to congregate at the far west end. Bicycling is also popular on the Seawall, although many cyclists take their two-wheelers for a detour through the East End Historic District. Swimmers can enjoy the gulf almost anywhere along the southern coast.

Shelling and Beachcombing

Although some are rare, several hundred species of shells can be found along the beaches of the Gulf of Mexico and the bays and salt marshes on the northern side of the island. Some shells are easier to find in certain

A bountiful assortment of shells awaits collectors along all of Galveston's beaches, especially at low tide.

seasons, although most varieties can be found in the spring. The largest number of shells (as well as driftwood) will be found at low tide, when the receding ocean water exposes more beach to search. If you begin your expedition as early in the day as possible, fewer of the treasures will have been picked over by other collectors.

Most experts agree that the best areas for shelling are along the beaches at the western end of the island and at Bolivar (reach it via the ferry), but shells are abundant almost everywhere. A large number of reference books about shells are available at the Rosenberg Library and a brief but informative pamphlet called *The Galveston Shell Club Presents Shells of Galveston Island* is available without charge at the Galveston Visitor Information Center. You can also see a collection of thousands of shells at Angelo's, a souvenir shop located at 3102 Avenue S (just off the beach at 31st Street). If you prefer to collect shells without getting your feet wet, you can buy them here at reasonable prices.

Saltwater Fishing

People under the age of 17 or over 65 do not need licenses to fish the waters of the gulf. For all others, a special saltwater sport fishing license costs only $1.25 and is good for three days. Licenses can be purchased at the Galveston County Courthouse, 722 Moody, and at bait shops and sporting goods stores all along the Seawall.

Numerous varieties of sport and food fish are abundant in the gulf waters off the southern shore of Galveston. Prevalent species are flounder, tarpon, catfish, speckled trout, croaker, and red fish. Although there are a number of commercial fishing sites on the island that charge a fee to anglers, free fishing piers (generally rocky jetties) are located along Seawall Boulevard at 10th, 17th, 30th, 37th, and 61st streets. Most of these piers are well-lighted for nighttime angling.

Bird Watching

Galveston's coastal birds include pelicans, gulls, egrets, cranes, and heron. Most can be spotted year-round. During the spring, migratory birds virtually inundate the island. "One of the best spots to sight these birds is in Kempner Park at 27th Street and Avenue O and High Island on Bolivar," reports longtime bird-watcher Allen Mueller. "After a storm, when the birds are returning across the gulf, you can sight every bird imaginable."

photo credits

Special thanks to the following people and organizations for supplying all of the photographs reproduced in this book.

> Greater Houston Convention and Visitors Center, pages 12, 18, 23, 31, 32, 39, 42, 44, 45, 48, 70, 71, 73, 79 (bottom), 81, 83, 88, 91, 97, 100, 107, 113 (bottom), 120, 131.
>
> National Parks Service, page, 20
>
> Houston Parks and Recreation Dept. (all photos by Chris Stone), pages 21, 47, 50, 52, 58, 59, 60, 62, 113 (top), 118.
>
> Houston Zoological Gardens, page, 24.
>
> U.S. Forest Service (photo by Dale Bounds), page 24.
>
> Contemporary Arts Museum (photo by Rick Gardner), page 33.
>
> Jim Hargrove, pages 36, 37, 67, 102, 108.
>
> Museum of Natural Science, page 41.
>
> National Aeronautics and Space Administration, pages 78, 79 (top).
>
> Voluntary Action Center of Houston and Harris County, page 88.
>
> Galveston News Bureau, pages 127, 130, 137.
>
> Galveston Historic Foundation, pages, 134, 136.

index

Abesti Gorgora V sculpture, 109
Allen Parkway Recreation Area, 48–49
Allen's Landing, 47–48
Almeda and Northwest malls exhibits, 116–17, 119–25
America mural, 109
American National Insurance Company Tower (Galveston), 128–29
American Red Cross classes, 66
Angelina National Forest, 25–26
Anheuser-Busch tour, 66
Annunciation Church, 66
Antioch Baptist Church, 66
Armand Bayou Wilderness Preserve, 17
Art galleries, 104–6
Artworks, outdoor, 106–9

Barker's Dam Telescope Tour, 67
Bay Area Park Boat Ride, 18
Bayou Bend Collection of the Museum of Fine Arts, 30–31
Beaches (Galveston), 130–32
Beachcombing (Galveston), 136–38
Bear Creek Park, 18–19
Bellaire Ethnic Folk Festival, 119

Bellaire Relics and Antiques Show, 120
Bird-watching (Galveston), 138
Big Creek Scenic Area, 19
Big Slough Canoe Trail, 26–28
Big Thicket National Preserve, 19–20
Blaffer Gallery, 31
Blessing of the Shrimp Fleet, 123
Bolivar Ferry, 129
Bonsai Society Show, 120
Brazosport Museum of Natural History, 32
Bromeliad Show and Sale, 122–23
Burke Baker Planetarium, 32

Cemeteries, 67–68
Christ Church Cathedral, 68
Cinco de Mayo, 121
Clayton Library, 94–95
Coca-Cola Bottling Plant tour, 69
Contemporary Arts Museum, 33
Crispin Building, 69
Custom Car Show, 118–19

Davy Crockett National Forest, 26–28
Dickens' Evening on the Strand, 127

East End Historic District (Galveston), 129–30
Edith Moore Sanctuary— Houston Audubon Society, 20–21
Eisenhower Park, 36

Family, The (sculpture), 109
Farmers Market Cooperative, 69
Fiestas Patrias, 123
Films, Miller Theatre free festival of, 114, 124. *Also see* Libraries, central; Houston Zoological Gardens; Strand Visitors Center.
Foley's Thanksgiving Day Parade, 125
Fort Bend County Museum, 34
4-C's National Recreation Trail, 28
Fourth of July celebrations, 122

Galveston, 128–38
  beaches, 130–32
  Visitor Information Center, 128
Galveston County Historical Museum, 132
Galleria shopping mall, 69–70
Geophysical Society of Houston Museum, 34
Gulf Coast Railroad Museum, 34

Hanging Tree, 71
Healer, The (sculpture), 110
Herman Brown Park, 49
Hermann Park, 49
Hermann Square, 64
Hilltop Herb Farm, 71
Historic downtown buildings, 74–77
Houston Amaryllis Show, 119
Houston Aquarium Society, 123
Houston Arboretum and Botanical Gardens, 21
Houston Baptist University, 103
Houston Baseball Museum, 34–35
Houston *Chronicle* newspaper tour, 82

Houston Civic Symphony, 115
Houston Federation of Garden Clubs Show, 117
Houston Festival, 117–18
Houston Fire Department, Station Number 1 tour, 71
Houston Folk Festival, 114, 123
Houston Garden Center and Rose Gardens, 22
Houston Heritage Society, 35–37
Houston Livestock and Rodeo Parade, 117
Houston Municipal Band, 115
Houston *Post* newspaper tour, 82
Houston Public Library, 38, 90–93
Houston Shakespearean Festival, 114, 122
Houston Symphony, 115
Houston underground tunnels, 72
Houston Zoological Gardens, 22–24

Imperial Sugar tour, 72
Industrial Arts Fair, 121
Intercontinental Airport, 77

Johnson Space Center, 77–80
June Tenth Blues Festival, 122

Kennedy Trading Post, 72

Lake Houston, 24
Lake Ratcliff, 26
Lapidary Society, 123
Libraries, public, 90–95
  branch, 92–93
  Central, 90–92
  Harris County, 93–94
Lone Star Hiking Trail, 28–29
Lyndon B. Johnson Space Center, 77–80

Martha Hermann Square, 64
Mecom Memorial Fountain, 106
Medical Center, 81

Memorial City Shopping Center
  Art Show, 116
Memorial Park, 49
Mercer Arboretum, 25
Messiah oratorio, 125
MG Car Show, 121–22
Miller Outdoor Theatre, 112–14
Mosquito Fleet (Galveston), 132
Museum of American
  Architecture and Decorative
  Arts, 38
Museum of Fine Arts, 38–39
  lawn sculptures, 109
Museum of Medical Science, 39–40
Museum of Natural Science, 40–41

NASA. *See* Lyndon B. Johnson
  Space Center.
Neches River, 26–28
Newspaper tours, 82

O'Kane Gallery, 41
Old Market Square, 82
Old Sixth Ward—Sabine
  Historical District, 82

Parks, city, 46–64
  basketball shelters, 57
  bicycle trails, 52–56
  classes, general, 58–59
  exertrails, 51–52
  recreation centers, 61
  senior citizen classes, 60
  swimming pools, 61–63
  tennis courts, 63–64
  therapeutic recreation, 59–60
Pasadena Historical Museum, 41–42
Peggy sculpture, 106
Pennzoil Place, 82–83
Pioneer Memorial Log Home, 83
Police Week, 121
Port of Houston, 83–84
Post Oak Central I, II, 84

R. A. Vines Environmental
  Science Center, 25

Rice University, 100–101
Rice University Museum, 42
Rosenberg Library (Galveston), 133
Rose Show, 125
Rothko Chapel, 42–43

Sabine Historical District, 82
St. Joseph Catholic Church, 82
St. Patrick's Day Parade, 117
Sam Houston Memorial
  Museum, 43
Sam Houston National Forest, 28–29
Sam Houston Park, 49
  candlelight tours, 125
Sam Houston statue, 106
Sam Houston touring vessel, 84
San Jacinto Battleground, 43
San Jacinto Day, 119–20
San Jacinto Monument and
  Museum of Texas History, 43–45
San Jacinto River, 24
Sauer's Sausage Company tour, 84
Saw Mill Hiking Trail, 26
Seawall, The (Galveston), 133
Shelling (Galveston), 136–38
Shopping malls and centers, 84–87
Small Games Tournament, 119
Society for the Prevention of
  Cruelty to Animals (SPCA), 87–88
SPCA Mutt Show, 121
Spindle Piece sculpture, 108
Strand, The (Galveston), 133–35
  Visitors Center, 135
Swimming pools, 61–63

Tennis courts, 63–64
Texas Heroes Monument
  (Galveston), 135
Texas Southern University, 101–3
Tranquility Park, 51
Trinity River Dam, 24
Tunnels, downtown, 72

University of Houston Central
    Campus, 97–99
    Beauty Bowl, 124
    concerts, 114
    Free Fair, 119, 123
University of St. Thomas, 103–4
U.S.S. *Texas* battleship, 45

Varner-Hogg Plantation State
    Park, 29
Voluntary Action Center of
    Houston and Harris County,
    88–89

Washington-on-the-Brazos
    State Park, 29
Westbury Square Sidewalk Art
    Sale, 124
William F. Hobby Airport, 89
William Marsh Rice sculpture,
    109
Woodcarver's Show, 124